T0330631

CULTURAL ENABLERS

When done well, implementing the principles found in the Cultural Enablers dimension of the *Shingo Model* leads to an organizational culture that assures a safe environment, places a special emphasis on the development of its people, and engages and empowers everyone in the pursuit of continuous improvement.

This sixth book of the Shingo Model series is laid out in a format similar to a Shingo workshop. You'll find chapters devoted to both of the principles, examples from organizations from around the world, an overview of key systems and ideal behaviors, and a few expanded case studies to aid your learning.

Cultural Enablers is designed to help all organizations on their journey toward excellence. You will better understand the concepts of respect and humility, and how these two principles can be brought to life through the creation of your own ideal behaviors. Although the systems listed here are not exhaustive, you'll discover an overview of a few systems that are critical to developing a world-class culture of continuous improvement that is characterized by high levels of engagement and daily problem-solving.

Shingo Model Series

Discover Excellence
Edited by Gerhard Plenert (2017)

Complex Management Systems and the Shingo Model
Authored by Rick Edgeman (2019)

Enterprise Alignment and Results
Edited by Chris Butterworth (2019)

Continuous Improvement
Edited by Larry Anderson, Dan Fleming, Bruce Hamilton & Pat Wardwell (2021)

Systems Design
Edited by Brent R. Allen & April A. Bosworth

Cultural Enablers
Edited by Michael Martyn & Eilish Henry (2023)

CULTURAL ENABLERS

RESPECT EVERY INDIVIDUAL AND LEAD WITH HUMILITY

Edited by

Michael Martyn and Eilish Henry

Routledge
Taylor & Francis Group

A PRODUCTIVITY PRESS BOOK

First published 2023
by Routledge
605 Third Avenue, New York, NY 10158

and by Routledge
4 Park Square, Milton Park, Abingdon, Oxon, OX14 4RN

Routledge is an imprint of the Taylor & Francis Group, an informa business

ISBN: 978-1-032-54576-9 (hbk)
ISBN: 978-1-032-54575-2 (pbk)
ISBN: 978-1-003-42551-9 (ebk)

DOI: 10.4324/9781003425519

Typeset in Minion
by Deanta Global Publishing Services, Chennai, India

To my wife, Jennifer, who first put up with my desire to be an author 10 years ago and still supports my passion for the work and my drive to share what I have learned with leaders and companies all over the world. To Shaun Barker and Jake Raymer, the first two guys I met at the Shingo Institute all those years ago. We have had so many great adventures together sharing the principles of operational excellence, piloting new workshops, leading assessments, and passionately helping organizations build cultures that inspire and motivate their people to excel. To my co-author, Eilish Henry, who continues to inspire me with her passion for the Shingo Model, *her experience helping companies' successful challenge for the prize, and her commitment to each of our clients. I am happy we had the opportunity to work together on this book and am proud of the work we have done over the years. Finally, during the 20 years I have associated with the Shingo Institute and the Shingo Prize, I have met some amazing people both in the Shingo Institute and in the 48 Shingo Award–recipient organizations we are honored to call our clients. The journey I have taken with them has been truly unique and I continue to grow in both my appreciation of the Shingo Model and my admiration of those who aspire to live its principles every day. To each of them I give my thanks.*

—Michael Martyn

To Noel, my husband of 50 years. Thank you for your unwavering support and forbearance during the many years I travelled across the globe to work with amazing people and organizations. Without you, the client examples in this book would not have been possible. Also, I have had the great fortune of working with the Shingo Institute for more than 13 years. And in that time, I have met so many great leaders, managers, and team members who have dedicated their lives to living the principles espoused in the Shingo Model. To all of you I offer my thanks for allowing me to be a part of your journey and inspiring me to do my best work.

—Eilish Henry

Contents

Acknowledgments xi

About the Editors xiii

Introduction xv

Chapter 1   Organizational Excellence and the Shingo Institute 1

Shigeo Shingo 1

Back to Basics 3

The Shingo Institute 4

The *Shingo Model* and the Shingo Prize 5

The Six Shingo Workshops 6

DISCOVER EXCELLENCE 7

SYSTEMS DESIGN 7

CULTURAL ENABLERS 8

CONTINUOUS IMPROVEMENT 8

ENTERPRISE ALIGNMENT 9

BUILD EXCELLENCE 9

The *Shingo Model* Series of Books 10

Chapter 2   The Cultural Enablers Dimension 11

The Importance of Culture 11

Research on Engagement 12

Balancing People and Process 15

Principles for Enabling Your Culture 15

Respect Every Individual 16

Lead with Humility 17

Cultural Enablers Supporting Concepts 18

Assure a Safe Environment 18

Develop People 19

Empower and Involve Everyone 20

A Learning Organization 21

Chapter 3   Respect Every Individual...23

Understanding the Principle.........................24
Owed and Earned Respect 25
Behavioral Benchmarks................................27
Examples of Ideal Behaviors 28
Principles in Action: Respect at AbbVie.....................31
The Lean Journey at AbbVie, Ballytivnan...............31
Shaping the Culture through Ideal Behaviors................32
The Importance of Safety 33
Results 34

Chapter 4   Lead with Humility...37

Understanding the Principle.........................37
Behavioral Benchmarks................................41
Examples of Ideal Behaviors 42
Principles in Action: Humility at Abbott Nutrition
One China 44
The Lean Journey at Abbott One China................45
Our Pledge Behaviors, Our Foundation.......... 46
Shaping Culture by Leading with Humility................47
The Importance of Development............................ 48
Leading with Humility through Mindful Leaders.............49
Results 50

Chapter 5   Enabling Culture at TESSEI 53

Enter Teruo Yabe 55
Changing Perceptions at TESSEI 57
Transforming the Role of Management 59
Getting Results...61
Reflections on Respect and Humility at TESSEI 63

Chapter 6   Systems That Support Cultural Enablers.......................65

What People Want from Culture 66
The Five Key Systems 68
System #1: Environmental, Health, and Safety 69

Example: Forest Tosara Baldoyle, Ireland 69
Example: Abbott in Ireland and the Croí an Óir
Program 70
Example: Hologic Costa Rica 73
System #2: Training and Development 74
Example: Viatris Damastown, Ireland 75
System #3: Continuous Improvement 77
Example: University of Washington, Seattle,
Washington 78
System #4: Coaching 79
Example: US Synthetic, Orem, Utah 80
System #5: Recognition 81
Example: OC Tanner, Salt Lake City, Utah 82
Best Practices for the "Appreciate Great in Culture
Cloud" Program 83

Chapter 7 Assessing the Cultural Enablers Dimension 85

Identify Your Ideal Behaviors 87
Example: Boston Scientific, Cork, Ireland 88
Developing an Effective Process 91
Example: University of Washington, Seattle,
Washington 93
Understanding Maturity 93

Chapter 8 The Impact of Enabling Your Culture 97

Transforming Culture at Abbott Diagnostics,
Longford, Ireland 98
The Journey to Excellence 99
The Five Systems at Abbott Longford 100
System #1: Environmental, Health, and Safety 100
System #2: Training and Development 103
System #3: Continuous Improvement 104
System #4: Coaching 105
System #5: Recognition 106
Results 106

Bibliography 109

Index 111

Acknowledgments

We want to thank a number of people who have played significant roles in helping us to write this book and for allowing us to share the story of their excellence journeys. Firstly, Sean Kelly, Global Program Manager, BB Divisional Business Excellence at Abbott Diagnostics, who played such an important part in the excellence journey of the Longford site. Sean not only allowed us to share his story of their journey, but he has been relentless in sharing with others the learning of the Longford site to the benefit of companies within the Abbott family and far beyond. The impact of his knowledge sharing can be seen in organizations across the globe.

Thanks also to Joseph Kumor, former Site Director at AbbVie, Ballytivnan, Sligo, Ireland, and now Senior Director Environmental Health Safety and Sustainability at AbbVie. Joe not only made a huge contribution to this book in sharing the story of AbbVie Sligo's journey to excellence, but he is also a true exemplar of the Shingo principles Respect Every Individual and Lead with Humility. Joe unfailingly credits others for the many successes his organization has achieved and is one of the most effective and respectful coaching leaders we have ever had the privilege of working with.

Thanks also to Fanny Chen, Divisional Vice President of Greater China Supply Chain and Strategic Relations at Abbott Nutrition. She is another truly inspirational leader who consistently puts the welfare of her people before all other considerations and who provides clear, respectful, and challenging direction and support for them.

To all our other clients who trusted us with your journey and to the other organizations we included in the book that have built great cultures, we thank you. Your examples, stories, and passion inspire all of us to continue on the path and strive to get better every day.

We are also grateful to Ken Snyder who asked us to write this book and entrusted us with generating a great outcome. He gave us creative license to bring the Cultural Enablers dimension of the *Shingo Model* to life by using our years of experience as well as examples from our clients. We believe this book is richer because of it.

Finally, thanks to our editor Jennifer Payne, for your patience, grace, and constant encouragement with the writing and editing of this book. It is a pleasure to work with you.

Michael Martyn
Eilish Henry

About the Editors

Michael Martyn

Michael Martyn is the Founder and President of SISU Consulting Group, an international consultancy that has supported more than 500 organizations in 22 countries. SISU Consulting Group is a Licensed Affiliate for the Shingo Institute and is responsible for training and developing certified Shingo trainers and examiners. Michael is based in Portland, Oregon, but travels extensively to support clients across the globe, including Europe, Latin America, and Asia. Over the past 20 years, Michael has also contributed to the development of the *Shingo Model* and the assessment framework, has received the Shingo Publication Award three times, and is a lifetime member of the Shingo Academy.

One of Michael's primary roles with SISU is the development of leaders at each level of the organization. In this role, Michael has trained and personally coached thousands of leaders through his live workshops, online development courses, executive coaching, and Coaching Camps. Michael has personally coached more than 200 organizations in implementing the principles of organizational excellence, including Baxter Healthcare, Boeing, Raytheon, Intermountain Healthcare, La-Z-Boy, OC Tanner, Daimler, University of Washington, Aera Energy, Boston Scientific, Christie Clinic, and Abbott.

His book *Own the Gap*, which received the Shingo Publication Award in 2013, sets out a clear and successful methodology for helping organizations translate the theory of the *Shingo Model* into reality and, by focusing on the four key systems, achieve world-class business results. The book has been used by thousands of leaders to understand how to design and implement a principle-based daily management system. In his most recent book, *Management for Omotenashi: Learning to Lead for Purpose, Passion, and Performance* (2022), Michael delivers a proven model for engaging people and delivering business results.

Prior to founding SISU, Michael worked in the private equity arena, successfully turning around companies in both manufacturing and service industries. It was during this time as a turnaround specialist that Michael was personally mentored in the principles of the Toyota Production System and refined his approach to driving business results by designing a management system that engages each member of the organization in team-based problem-solving toward customer-centric goals.

Eilish Henry

Eilish Henry is the Director for Europe of SISU Consulting Group. She is experienced in business delivery, organizational change in particular cultural change, including both design and implementation. Her focus is on ensuring the sustainability of improvements by securing real "buy-in" and ownership at all levels of the client business. She is a Shingo examiner and is highly experienced in assessing organizations against the enterprise excellence frameworks. She has worked closely with a number of client organizations to support them in developing their own assessment frameworks and to develop their teams of internal assessors. Eilish has completed more than 150 formal Shingo assessments and is a lifetime member of the Shingo Academy.

She was the first Shingo global coach (which has since been discontinued) and certified facilitator in Europe, and over the past 13 years she has taught more than 100 Shingo workshops and has supported 48 organizations to achieve all levels of Shingo recognition. This includes all but one of Ireland's Shingo Award recipients. In particular, she has supported 12 out of the 20 most recent Shingo Prize recipients.

She has worked with a huge range of organizations across the globe and in multiple sectors to help them build their cultures of excellence. In 2004, she was awarded the Order of the British Empire (OBE) for her work in leading large cultural change programs in the UK public sector.

Introduction

This book is the culmination of 20 years of working with the Shingo Institute. During that time, I (Michael Martyn) have had the pleasure of wearing just about every hat Shingo had to offer. I started out as a Shingo examiner, became a team lead, served as the executive director of the Northwest Shingo Prize (Washington, Oregon, and California), trained examiners, conducted the first Shingo assessments in healthcare and the Department of Defense, wrote curriculum for Shingo workshops, served on the Executive Board and the Board of Examiners, became an adjunct professor for the Shingo MBA program, and most currently, serve as a Licensed Affiliate and a Senior Curriculum Advisor.

I first met my partner, Eilish Henry, in 2008 at a Shingo Conference when she asked me about my role as the executive director of the Northwest Shingo Prize (back when the Shingo Institute administered regional prizes), my experience as an examiner, and my thoughts on helping organizations challenge for the prize. We kept in touch over the ensuing years, and I always felt a bond with her personally and admired her approach to working with clients. When the opportunity arose to have her join SISU Consulting Group in 2015, I took it. The rest is history. Eilish has been our director of Europe ever since and has helped hundreds of organizations implement principle-based daily management systems and successfully achieve Shingo recognition.

Our work with clients covers the entire *Shingo Model* as well as designing systems, but I believe our clients would tell you that our real specialty is engaging people and coaching leaders in creating a culture of respect and humility. Over the years, we have seen many changes to the *Shingo Model* as well as to the definition of what constitutes ideal behavior best practices. What has not changed is the focus on building a culture, as seen through the behaviors of leaders, managers, and team members. When done well, implementing the principles found in the Cultural Enablers dimension of the *Shingo Model* leads to an organizational culture that assures a safe environment, places a special emphasis on the development of its people, and engages and empowers everyone in the pursuit of continuous improvement.

This book is laid out in a format similar to a Shingo workshop. There are chapters devoted to each of the two principles, examples from our clients, an overview of key systems and ideal behaviors, and a few expanded case studies to aid you in your learning. Following is a brief summary of the content contained in each chapter.

- **Chapter 1** includes a short history of Shigeo Shingo and the Shingo Prize. It also reviews the elements of the *Shingo Model* and the current Shingo workshops.
- **Chapter 2** provides an overview of the Cultural Enablers dimension of the *Shingo Model*. The current gap in leadership effectiveness and team member engagement is discussed and the two principles are introduced alongside each of the three supporting concepts.
- **Chapter 3** is devoted to the principle of Respect Every Individual. In this chapter, we define the principle, discuss what respect means in the context of a great culture, and explore behavioral benchmarks and ideal behaviors. We end the chapter with a case study of Senior Director Joseph Kumor and his Shingo journey at AbbVie.
- **Chapter 4** dives into the principle, Lead with Humility. As with the chapter on respect, we define the behaviors, explore the characteristics of a humble leader, and review the behavior benchmarks and ideal behaviors. This chapter ends with a case study of senior leader Fanny Chen and her Shingo journey at Abbott Nutrition Supply Chain One China.
- **Chapter 5** is a detailed review of one of the case studies used in the CULTURAL ENABLERS workshop. The case study is on TESSEI and illustrates how their former chairman, Teruo Yabe, built a culture of respect and humility based on redefining the role of leaders, rebranding what it means to be a cleaner at TESSEI, and reimagining the customer experience.
- **Chapter 6** builds upon the previous chapters and reviews the importance of systems in enabling a culture of respect and humility. It also reviews the key systems every organization should have in order to achieve excellence. Each of the systems discussed in this chapter includes an example of an organization's efforts that will help illustrate what the system looks like when it is done well. It will also help inspire you to implement it in your own organization.

- **Chapter 7** focuses on the assessment process and how to understand the maturity of your culture through the eyes of an examiner. We discuss creating ideal behaviors, designing an effective assessment process, and using objective criteria based on the approach used by the Shingo Institute.
- **Chapter 8** is the culmination of the entire book and discusses the impact of implementing the principles of respect and humility in an organization. In this chapter, we use an expanded example from Abbott Diagnostics Longford, recipient of the Shingo Prize in 2016, as one of the best examples of an organization who has selflessly helped others through the sharing of their best practices and lessons learned.

Now, a quick note on how best to use this book on your journey to organizational excellence. It is important to remember that this book represents an introduction to the Cultural Enablers dimension of the *Shingo Model*. As such, we highly suggest that you devote more study to the concepts of respect and humility and how these two principles can be brought to life through the creation of your own ideal behaviors. Second, we have provided you with an overview of five systems that we believe are critical to developing a world-class culture of continuous improvement that is characterized by high levels of engagement and daily problem-solving. This list is not exhaustive, and it could be argued that your real challenge is determining how to best embed respect and humility in each system you employ as opposed to thinking of certain systems as being critical for enabling your culture. Finally, while we feel strongly that each example included here will be both informative and inspiring, we caution you from trying to copy the example straight from the book. In each of the organizations we highlight here, co-creating the system with the input of leaders, managers, and team members was critical to its success. In addition, the designing of a system organically from the ground up turns out to be "the secret sauce" (if there is one).

That being said, we hope you enjoy this book and that it serves its purpose in helping you on your organization's journey to excellence.

1

Organizational Excellence and the Shingo Institute

Too many organizations are failing to be competitive, not because they cannot solve problems, but because they cannot sustain the solution. They haven't realized that tradition supersedes tools, no matter how good they are. Success requires a sustainable shift in behaviors and culture, and that needs to be driven by a shift in the systems that motivate those behaviors.*

—Gerhard Plenert

SHIGEO SHINGO

In 1988, a Japanese industrial engineering consultant and author, Shigeo Shingo (shown in Figure 1.1), bestowed his name on the "North American Shingo Prizes for Excellence in Manufacturing." While recognized for his genius by only a few individuals in the West, Shingo was highly regarded in Japan as a co-creator of the concepts, tools, and philosophy of the Toyota Production System (TPS). He was also the author of 18 books on the subject.

Vernon Buhler, a director of Utah State University's (USU) Partners in Business program, was an early advocate of Shingo's teachings. It was Buhler who persuaded Shingo to accept an honorary doctorate in 1988 and to add his name to the Prize for Excellence in Manufacturing.

---

* Gerhard Plenert, *Discover Excellence: An Overview of the Shingo Model and Its Guiding Principles* (Boca Raton, FL: CRC, 2018), 1.

DOI: 10.4324/9781003425519-1

FIGURE 1.1

Shigeo Shingo receives an honorary doctorate at Utah State University in Logan, Utah, in 1988.

Shingo wanted the prizes, which were administered by the Jon M. Huntsman School of Business at Utah State University, to be awarded each year to organizations and academics whose work exemplified the best of Shingo's teachings. The prizes were to be awarded in three categories: (1) large businesses of more than 500 employees, (2) small businesses of 500 or fewer employees, and (3) academics who made scholarly contributions to the body of knowledge surrounding Shingo's work.

The mission of the Shingo Prize was, as it is today, to recognize successful implementation of Shingo's ideas as examples of best practice for others to follow. Shingo wanted "to give back to North America" for what he himself had learned from his "teacher's teachers." These included Frank and Lillian Gilbreth, William Taylor, and Henry Ford.

With a $50,000 donation from Norman Bodek, founder and former president of Productivity Press, and generous support from Utah State University (USU), the fledgling Shingo Prize presented its first award in 1989 at the 14th Annual Partners in Business Conference in Logan, Utah. By that time, several of Shingo's books had been translated into English from Japanese. This afforded organizations throughout the world the benefit of his incredible tools, such as SMED (single-minute exchange of dies) and poka-yoke (mistake proofing). Perhaps even more valuable in Shingo's teachings were his observations on human nature and development, although the latter points were largely overlooked in favor of his tools in the early days of the Shingo Prize.

By 2008, Shingo's work and the significance of TPS beyond manufacturing became apparent to the Shingo Prize administrators. They expanded the scope of the Shingo Prize beyond North America and also made the Prize available to participants from non-manufacturing entities. The rebranded "Shingo Prize for Operational Excellence" was adopted. It included two additional significant but lesser levels of the award: The silver and bronze medallions. Around this time, Prize administrators recognized the need and responsibility to provide a deeper understanding of the conceptual and philosophical foundations of Shingo's tools and methods, the know-why behind the know-how, as Shingo described them in his teachings.

BACK TO BASICS

The term *Lean* was first introduced in 1990 in the book *The Machine That Changed the World: The Story of Lean Production*. In it, the authors, James Womack, Daniel Jones, and Daniel Roos, describe Lean as a manufacturing system that is based on the principles employed in the Toyota Production System (TPS). They wrote:

> Lean ... is "lean" because it uses less of everything compared with mass production—half the human effort in the factory, half the manufacturing space, half the investment in tools, half the engineering hours to develop a new product in half the time. Also, it requires keeping far less than half the inventory on site, results in many fewer defects, and produces a greater and ever-growing variety of products.*

In the intervening years, the philosophy of Lean has gone through numerous iterations. It stresses the maximization of customer value while simultaneously minimizing waste. The goal of Lean is to create increased value for customers while simultaneously utilizing fewer resources. Countless organizations have, at one time or another, begun a Lean journey or implemented an improvement

---

* J.P. Womack, et al. *The Machine That Changed the World: The Story of Lean Production—Toyota's Secret Weapon in the Global Car Wars That Is Now Revolutionizing World Industry* (New York, NY: Simon & Schuster, Inc., 1990), 14.

initiative of some sort. At the foundation of these initiatives are a plethora of tools (over 100) that seem to promise exciting new results. They are utilized to optimize the flow of products and services throughout an entire value stream as they horizontally flow through an organization.

While many organizations may initially see significant improvements, far too many of these initiatives meet disappointing ends. Leaders quickly find that tools such as Six Sigma, SMED, 5S, and JIT are not independently capable of effecting lasting change.

THE SHINGO INSTITUTE

The Shingo Institute has assessed organizations in various industries around the world. The Institute has seen first-hand how some organizations have been able to sustain their improvement results, while far too many have experienced such a decline. In fact, initially, the Shingo Prize focused on tools and systems and how those tools and systems drive results. The Prize was originally given out based on these results.

But when far too many Shingo Prize recipient organizations reverted to their old ways, the Shingo Institute realized there was a big piece missing in its earlier model of organizational excellence based only on systems, tools, and short-term results. So, the Shingo Institute set out to determine the key difference between short-lived successes and sustainable results. Over time, the Institute discovered a common theme: The difference between sustainable and unsustainable effort is centered on the ability of an organization to ingrain into its culture timeless and universal principles, rather than rely on the superficial implementation of tools and programs. This is because principles help people understand the "why" behind the "how" and the "what." Sustainable results depend upon the degree to which an organization's culture is aligned to specific, guiding principles rather than depending solely on tools, programs, or initiatives.

The Shingo Institute discovered that what was lacking was sustained superior performance, a sustained culture of excellence and innovation, and a sustained environment for social and ecological leadership. To really make progress in a journey to organizational excellence, we must have long-term sustainability. Change could no longer be something that happened once a year during a Lean event. Instead, organizations need to constantly look for improvement opportunities.

THE *SHINGO MODEL* AND THE SHINGO PRIZE

To best illustrate its new findings, the Shingo Institute developed the *Shingo Model*™, the accompanying *Shingo Guiding Principles*, and the *Three Insights of Organizational Excellence*™. The principles are timeless and universal. They apply to all cultures and they do not change over time. They govern consequences and provide a solid foundation for developing a roadmap to excellence (Figure 1.2).

Now, the Shingo Prize is awarded to organizations that have robust key systems driving behavior closer to ideal, as informed by the principles of organizational excellence, and measured by strong key performance indicator and key behavioral indicator trends and levels. Shingo Prize recipients show

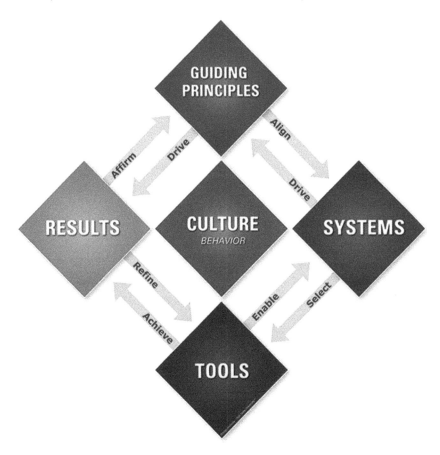

FIGURE 1.2
Shingo Model.

the greatest potential for sustainability as measured by the frequency, intensity, duration, scope, and role of the behaviors evident in the organizational culture. The Shingo Prize has become the global standard for organizational excellence. As an effective way to benchmark progress toward excellence, organizations throughout the world may apply and challenge for the Prize. Recipients receiving this recognition fall into three categories: Shingo Prize, the Shingo Silver Medallion, and the Shingo Bronze Medallion.

Most organizations do not wait until they believe they might qualify for the Shingo Prize to challenge for it. They challenge for the Prize so they can have a team of organizational excellence experts visit their company and evaluate their performance. They use the *Shingo Model* and the assessment process to measure themselves as they work toward the highest standard of excellence in the world. They use the guidelines to direct them, to inspire them, and to hold themselves responsible.

Over the years, the Shingo Institute's scope has expanded to include various educational offerings, a focus on research, and a growing international network of Shingo Licensed Affiliates. The *Shingo Model* is the primary subject of the Institute's popular workshops and publications. These materials have been developed to share throughout the world so organizations can learn how to create a sustainable cultural shift, which will ultimately lead to organizational excellence.

Similarly, volunteer Shingo examiners, who are international experts in all aspects of organizational excellence, focus on determining the degree to which the *Shingo Guiding Principles* are evident in the behavior of every team member in an organization. They observe behavior and the evidence of it to determine the frequency, intensity, duration, scope, and role of current behavior measured against the desired principle-based behaviors. They observe the degree to which leaders are focused on principles and culture, and the degree to which managers are focused on aligning systems to drive ideal behaviors at all levels.

THE SIX SHINGO WORKSHOPS

As part of its educational offerings, the Shingo Institute offers a series of six workshops that are designed to help participants understand the *Shingo Model*, its guiding principles, and its insights. Ultimately, these workshops help participants strive for excellence within their respective organizations. Each of the workshops is described in the following section.

DISCOVER EXCELLENCE

This foundational, two-day workshop introduces the *Shingo Model*, the *Shingo Guiding Principles*, and the *Three Insights of Organizational Excellence*. With active discussions and on-site learning at a host organization, this program is a highly interactive experience. It is designed to make learning meaningful and immediately applicable as participants discover how to release the latent potential in an organization to achieve organizational excellence. It provides the basic understanding needed in all Shingo workshops; therefore, it is a prerequisite to all the other Shingo workshops. During this workshop, participants will learn and understand the *Shingo Model*, discover the *Three Insights of Organizational Excellence*, and explore how the *Shingo Guiding Principles* inform ideal behaviors that ultimately lead to sustainable results. They will also understand the behavioral assessment process through an interactive case study and on-site learning.

SYSTEMS DESIGN

This two-day workshop integrates classroom and on-site experiences at a host facility to build upon the knowledge and experience gained in the DISCOVER workshop and focuses on the Systems and Tools diamonds in the *Shingo Model*. It begins by explaining that all work in an organization is the outcome of a system. Systems must be designed to create a specific end objective; otherwise, they evolve on their own. Systems drive the behavior of people, and variation in behavior leads to variation in results. Organizational excellence requires well-designed systems to drive ideal behaviors that are required to produce sustainable results. During this workshop, participants will discover three types of essential systems and explore five required communication tools for each system. They will also learn how to create and use system maps and understand system standard work and how it drives improvement.

CULTURAL ENABLERS

This two-day workshop integrates classroom and on-site experiences at a host facility to build upon the knowledge and experience gained in the DISCOVER and SYSTEMS workshops. It takes participants deeper into the *Shingo Model* by focusing on the principles identified in the Cultural Enablers dimension: Respect Every Individual and Lead with Humility.

Cultural Enablers principles make it possible for people in an organization to engage in the transformation journey, progress in their understanding, and build a culture of organizational excellence. Organizational excellence cannot be achieved through top-down directives or piecemeal implementation of tools. It requires a widespread organizational commitment. The Cultural Enablers workshop will help participants define ideal behaviors and the systems that drive those behaviors using behavioral benchmarks.

CONTINUOUS IMPROVEMENT

This two- or three-day workshop integrates classroom and on-site experiences at a host facility to build upon the knowledge and experience gained in the DISCOVER and SYSTEMS workshops. It begins by teaching participants how to clearly define value through the eyes of their customers. It continues the discussion about ideal behaviors, fundamental purpose, and behavioral benchmarks and takes participants deeper into the *Shingo Model* by focusing on the principles identified in the Continuous Improvement dimension: Seek Perfection, Embrace Scientific Thinking, Focus on Process, Assure Quality at the Source, and Improve Flow & Pull. The CONTINUOUS IMPROVEMENT workshop will deepen participants' understanding of the relationship between behaviors, systems, and principles and how they drive results.

ENTERPRISE ALIGNMENT

This two-day workshop integrates classroom and on-site experiences at a host facility to build upon the knowledge and experience gained in the DISCOVER and SYSTEMS workshops. It takes participants deeper into the *Shingo Model* by focusing on the principles identified in the Enterprise Alignment dimension: Think Systemically, Create Constancy of Purpose, and Create Value for the Customer.

To succeed, organizations must develop management systems that align work and behaviors with principles and direction in ways that are simple, comprehensive, actionable, and standardized. Organizations must get results. Creating value for customers is ultimately accomplished through the effective alignment of every value stream in an organization. The ENTERPRISE ALIGNMENT workshop continues the discussion around defining ideal behaviors and the systems that drive them.

BUILD EXCELLENCE

This two-day capstone workshop integrates classroom and on-site experiences at a host facility to solidify the knowledge and experience gained from the previous five Shingo workshops. The BUILD EXCELLENCE workshop demonstrates the integrated execution of systems that drive behavior toward the ideal as informed by the principles in the *Shingo Model*. The workshop helps to develop a structured approach to execute a cultural transformation. It builds upon a foundation of principles, using tools that already exist within many organizations. Participants will learn how to build systems that drive behavior that will consistently deliver desired results.

In this final Shingo workshop, participants will learn how to design or create a system, guided by the *Shingo Model*, that changes behaviors to close gaps and drives results closer to organizational goals and purpose. They will answer the question: "How do I get everyone on board?" They will understand the relationship between behaviors, systems, and principles, and how they drive results. Finally, participants will learn how Key Behavioral Indicators (KBIs) drive Key Performance Indicators (KPIs), and how this leads to excellent results.

THE *SHINGO MODEL* SERIES OF BOOKS

In conjunction with the Shingo Workshop series, the Shingo Institute has set out to publish six books that are specifically focused on the primary components of the *Shingo Model* and its guiding principles. This book, *Cultural Enablers*, is one of the books in the series. Four others, *Systems Design*, *Continuous Improvement*, *Discover Excellence*, and *Enterprise Alignment*, have already been published.

In all of these efforts, the focus at the Shingo Institute is unique in the world. Its work is the most rigorous way to determine if an organization is fundamentally improving over the long term. Its goal is to help every organization reach excellence, wherever it may be along its path.

2

The Cultural Enablers Dimension

People will understand something if the reasoning is explained to them. But understanding by itself will never get things put into practical operation. People will not swing into action until they are convinced by the arguments. Understanding is a function of reason, whereas conviction is an emotion.[*]

—*Shigeo Shingo*

THE IMPORTANCE OF CULTURE

Upon closer look at the *Shingo Model*, one can see that the Cultural Enablers dimension sits at the base of the principles pyramid (Figure 2.1). While many people incorrectly assume that the size of each dimension in the pyramid is making a deeper statement on the importance of each dimension relative to the others, it is interesting to note the position and size of Cultural Enablers. You will often hear it expressed that "culture is the foundation upon which to build your systems and achieve operational excellence." Similarly, *The Shingo Model* booklet states, "Cultural enablers are at the foundation of the pyramid because they focus on the foundation of an organization: its people."[†] Regardless of whether you agree with the above statements, we have found that cultural enablers are so important to achieving sustained excellence that they should be considered bedrock because they enable all the other systems to drive behavior closer to ideal. The better you design your cultural enabling

---

[*] Shigeo Shingo, *The Sayings of Shigeo Shingo: Key Strategies for Plant Improvement*, trans. Andrew P. Dillon (Cambridge, MA: Productivity Press, 1987), 129.
[†] Shingo Institute, *The Shingo Model*, version 14.6 (Logan, UT: Utah State University, 2021), 16.

DOI: 10.4324/9781003425519-2   *11*

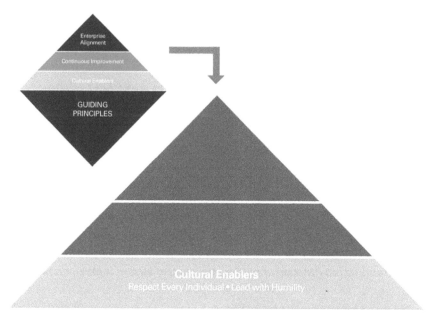

FIGURE 2.1
Cultural enablers are at the foundation of the pyramid because they focus on the foundation of an organization: its people.

systems, the more positive impact they will have on all other systems, and the better your results and the happier your people. Cultural enablers are one of the keys to cultural sustainability.

At the heart of the *Shingo Model's* definition of enabling a culture is to create an environment that both inspires and engages its people. Regardless of the plans you have for organizational growth, efficient systems, and sustained profitability, without a committed workforce willing to own and solve problems every day, your efforts will fall short of your potential. Therefore, focusing on implementing the principles found in the Cultural Enablers dimension of the *Shingo Model* is paramount in your journey to excellence. The impact of a poor culture characterized by a lack of engagement and ownership of one's contribution to work has been well documented.

RESEARCH ON ENGAGEMENT

The importance of the *Shingo Model* and, more specifically, the Cultural Enablers dimension is reinforced by the research Gallup* has done since

---

* Jim Clifton and Jim Harter, *It's the Manager: Moving from Boss to Coach* (Gallup Press, 2019).

1996 with its Q12 model, working with millions of employees in 195 countries and focusing on global workforce engagement scores. In its most recent research, Gallup studied more than 1.8 million employees in 230 organizations across 49 industries in 73 countries.* The results of Gallup surveys have remained largely unchanged since the first study was conducted more than 24 years ago. An overwhelming percentage of employees are not engaged at work and the lack of engagement is costing companies trillions of dollars per year. In fact, on a global scale, some 85 percent of employees are either not engaged or actively disengaged and the cost of lost productivity from this segment of the workforce is $7 trillion annually.

Why is Gallup's research important to our discussion of the Cultural Enablers dimension? First, enabling your culture is directly related to your success at leveraging the principles of respect and humility to improve engagement, ownership, and desire for continuous improvement. Second, since the fundamental role of leaders is to get results, an improvement in engagement has been consistently correlated with improved performance in an organization across a variety of metrics. Take the following examples from Gallup's research:

41 percent lower absenteeism
20 percent fewer defects
24 percent less turnover (high TO)
10 percent higher customer ratings
59 percent less turnover (low TO)
17 percent higher productivity
70 percent fewer safety incidents
20 percent higher sales
58 percent fewer patient safety incidents
21 percent higher profitability

Finally, and maybe more importantly, Gallup's research matters to our discussion on cultural enablers because of the bombshell it dropped as the single largest cause for the lack of engagement. While there are numerous factors that influence engagement scores, Gallup concluded that the largest single factor to account for the variance in team engagement is

---

* Ibid.

solely due to the manager (70 percent). When an organization talks about the importance of culture and their goal of building a world-class culture of continuous improvement, they are really speaking of their leader's skills and capabilities as they relate to creating an environment that engages their people. Since the *Shingo Model* is explicit about the need to define ideal behaviors for each level in the organization (leaders, managers, and team members), helping managers learn what improves or detracts from engagement is paramount.

What's more, when Gallup explored the data further, they found some startling statistics on current manager capabilities. Only 30 percent of current managers are great and skilled at engaging their team members. Fifty percent are "there," and 20 percent are "lousy." Further, only 21 percent of employees strongly agree that they are managed in a way that motivates them to do outstanding work.

What do people want from their leaders? Some things have changed little since Gallup first started polling. People want clear and consistent expectations at work, they want to be cared for as individuals, and they want to have their manager encourage and support their growth and development. However, as the workforce has changed over the years, so too have team members' expectations of their managers and organizations changed to reflect the times. More specifically, today's millennials are characterized by their challenging views on work, development, management, and coaching. Gallup summarized their changing preferences into six key areas:

1. Millennials want purpose, not just a paycheck.
2. Millennials want development, not job satisfaction.
3. Millennials want coaches, not bosses.
4. Millennials want ongoing conversations, not annual reviews.
5. Millennials don't want a manager who fixates on their weaknesses.
6. For millennials, work is their life, not just a job.

In addition, the value placed on money has decreased while the desire for purpose and meaning at work has increased. The definition of a "great job" no longer means making more money. A great job now equates to making a living wage and having a manager or team leader who encourages development. When people have the opportunity to find purpose in their work, pursue development, and integrate their work with their life, their engagement rises and their loyalty to the organization flourishes.

BALANCING PEOPLE AND PROCESS

It is clear from Gallup's research that inspiring and engaging your people takes more than a well-crafted mission statement and competitive compensation package. Today's workers want an organization they can believe in. They no longer separate their life from what they do at work, and they want to align their personal purpose with the purpose of the organization. Development is high on their list of goals, and when it comes to leaders, they want to have someone who engages them in a dialogue and balances feedback on strengths and weaknesses. Above all, they are looking for a leader who coaches and mentors them rather than tells and directs.

These findings bring us back to a critical theme of the *Shingo Model* and the reason the Cultural Enablers dimension is foundational to your success. Regardless of how much you focus your attention on improving process, if you do not engage your people and align their purpose and passion, the performance will not follow. In order to achieve industry-leading results that sustain over time, you must realize that enabling a culture of respect and humility cannot be an afterthought. It cannot be relegated to the back burner while you focus on your "mission critical strategy and tactics." Learning to lead through respect and humility is the determining factor in effectively aligning the enterprise, continuously improving processes, and generating business results.

PRINCIPLES FOR ENABLING YOUR CULTURE

The Cultural Enablers dimension of the *Shingo Model* contains two principles: Respect Every Individual and Lead with Humility. The first thing to notice is how the principles are stated. Like every principle in the *Shingo Model*, the concepts of respect and humility are expressed actively—each one starts with a verb. Because the principles are stated in terms of "what we must do" rather than "what the principle is," a tone is immediately set. The use of active language not only reinforces the importance of the principle but also defines the role leaders must play in bringing the principles to life. Acknowledging both the need for the principle and the commitment of leadership to live it every day is critical to your success.

Second, as you learn more about enabling your culture through the implementation of principle-based behaviors, you will see how many of the behaviors that are attributed to the two principles are often interchangeable in the minds of people. It is not uncommon for people in workshops or at client sites to debate whether a specific behavior is demonstrating respect for every individual or leading with humility. As the concepts of respect and humility are often intertwined, the focus should not be determining which principle informs each behavior. Rather, the focus should be on ensuring that ideal behavior that is informed by respecting people and leading with humility is the focal point in a cultural transformation.

Let's take a closer look at the principles contained in the Cultural Enablers dimension.

RESPECT EVERY INDIVIDUAL

> *Respect must become something that is deeply felt for and by every person in an organization. Respect for every individual naturally includes respect for customers, suppliers, the community, and society in general. Individuals are energized when this type of respect is demonstrated. Most team members will say that to be respected is the most important thing they want from their employer. When people feel respected, they give far more than their hands; they give their minds and hearts as well.**

When we look at the description that the *Shingo Model* provides us with, there are numerous areas of focus. First, respect is not only meant to be applied universally in the organization (to every individual). For the principle of respect to enable an engaged culture, it must be *felt* deeply by each person. Thus, it is not enough for us to say that we value respect

---

* Shingo Institute, *The Shingo Model,* 17.

in our organization or that we lead in a respectful way. Regardless of our efforts, systems, or structures to ensure respect, if every person does not feel respected, we have not achieved our goal. The second item to notice is that respect does not merely correspond to the leaders, managers, and team members of the organization. Respect for every individual also extends to customers, suppliers, the community, and society in general. The respect shown for each of the organization's stakeholders and the communicant and society at large are a source of pride and motivation for employees. Finally, respect is what people want most from their jobs, and if they get it, they will do more than just their job; they will take ownership of their contribution and give their minds and hearts as well.

> Respect commands itself and can neither be given nor withheld when it is due.*

LEAD WITH HUMILITY

> *One common trait among leading practitioners of organizational excellence is a sense of humility. Humility is an enabling principle that precedes learning and improvement. A leader's willingness to seek input, listen carefully, and continuously learn creates an environment where team members feel respected and energized and will give freely of their creative abilities. Improvement is only possible when people are willing to acknowledge their vulnerability and abandon bias and prejudice in their pursuit of a better way.†*

The description of humility focuses heavily on the role of leaders and the ideal behaviors they demonstrate when leading effectively. First, it is important to understand that leading with humility is strongly associated with active listening and adopting an attitude where leaders are consistent in their desire to seek the input of others and integrate the best thinking and ideas the organization can create. This openness to the ideas of others creates an environment where people feel valued for their contribution and trusted in their opinions and their ability to solve important problems

---

* Eldridge Cleaver, *Soul on Ice* (New York, NY: Dell Publishing, 1968), 97.
† Shingo Institute, *The Shingo Model,* 18.

and drive results. Finding the right balance between leading people and acknowledging mistakes and changing course requires vulnerability and a strong sense of self. Finally, leading with humility means committing to creating a learning environment where challenging goals, ownership of problems, and continuous improvement are the hallmarks of daily work.

> When we treat people merely as they are, they will remain as they are. When we treat them as if they were what they should be, they will become what they should be.*

CULTURAL ENABLERS SUPPORTING CONCEPTS

The supporting concepts of the Cultural Enablers principles help leaders understand these principles at a deeper level and work together to ensure that the culture they create embodies respect and humility in all they do. Each supporting concept also serves to help bridge the gap between the principle itself and the ideal behaviors that leaders define and strive to achieve. Simply put, an environment that demonstrates respect for every individual is one that assures a safe environment and focuses time and energy to develop its people. Similarly, an environment that demonstrates humility in its leadership style empowers and involves everyone and strives to be a learning organization. Following are the descriptions the Shingo Institute provides to help us understand the concept and determine how each concept contributes to a culture of respect and humility.

ASSURE A SAFE ENVIRONMENT

> *There is no greater measure of respect for the individual than creating a work environment that promotes both the health and safety of employees and the protection of the environment and the surrounding community. Environmental and safety systems embody a philosophical and cultural*

---

* Thomas S. Monson, "With Hand and Heart," (speech, General Conference of The Church of Jesus Christ of Latter-day Saints, Salt Lake City, UT, October 3, 1971).

commitment that begins with leadership. When leadership is committed, the organization creates and supports appropriate systems and behaviors. In short, safety is first.*

Creating a safe environment is the number one priority of leaders whose goal is to have an engaged and passionate culture of daily problem solvers. If people do not feel safe, they do not feel valued. If they do not feel safe, they do not feel free to think creatively about improving their work. Most importantly, if they do not feel safe, they do not feel a connection to the organization, which leads to a lack of ownership and even apathy. In the past, when we spoke of assuring a safe environment, people primarily referred to an environment free from physical harm. More recently, the importance of creating psychological safety has also become a priority. Leaders striving to enable a world-class culture must focus on both the physical and psychological safety of their people.

In addition to the concept of personal safety, ensuring a safe environment also includes a focus on protecting the environment and contributing to the surrounding community. At an increasing rate, people want to be proud of the organization they work for, and they want to be aligned with the organization's purpose and vision for the future. A key component of what millennials are looking for in an employer is an organization that focuses on more than profits. They are looking for an organization that wants to contribute to the greater good that includes being stewards of environments and contributors to local communities. If an organization's leaders can balance their commitment to the customers with care for the community, they will find a winning combination for both engaging their people and improving their performance.

DEVELOP PEOPLE

People development has emerged as an important and powerful cultural enabler and goes hand-in-hand with principles of organizational excellence. Through people development, the organization creates "new scientists" who will drive future improvement. People development is more involved than

---

* Shingo Institute, *The Shingo Model*, 18.

simple classroom training. It includes hand-on experiences where people can discover new ideas in a way that creates personal insight and a shift in mind-set and behavior.*

The supporting concept of developing people has two primary points of focus in the *Shingo Model*. First, while people can be developed in any number of topics or fields of study, with respect to organizational excellence, the primary goal is to develop them into problem solvers, or "scientists." When empowered and engaged, this army of problem solvers relentlessly pushes the organization to new heights through continuous daily improvement.

Second, for development to be truly impactful and lead to a sustained change in behavior, it must be experiential. That is not to say that classroom training is not an important part of a well-rounded training and development program. Far too often, though, organizations only equate development with classroom training. The ability for people to grow and embrace new ways of thinking and habits is not developed in the classroom. To truly develop people, we must place them in situations and scenarios where they are challenged and trusted to apply new learning and to experience both successes and failures that come from experimentation.

> We know culture is driven by leaders. But expressing to leaders what they do (huddles, standard work, strategy deployment …) in Lean culture often results in missing the point and represents perfunctory motion. We get better when we teach them how to think or be. Be humble, be respectful, seek perfection, focus on customer value, think systemically, think scientifically, flow value, focus on the process …. That certainly is more effective.[†]

EMPOWER AND INVOLVE EVERYONE

For an organization to be competitive, the full potential of every individual must be realized. People are the only organizational asset that has an

---

[*] Shingo Institute, *The Shingo Model*, 19.
[†] Eric Pope, Vice President, US Synthetic, quoted in Michael Martyn, *Management for Omotenashi: Learning to Lead for Purpose, Passion, and Performance* (Portland, OR: SISU Press, 2022), i.

infinite capacity to appreciate in value. The challenges of competing in global markets are so great that success can only be achieved when every person at every level of the organization is able to continuously innovate and improve. Elimination of barriers to that innovation becomes the responsibility of management.[*]

Empowering and involving everyone speaks directly to the gap in engagement Gallup has consistently found in its research. For people to be engaged, they must be trusted to contribute and challenged to participate in both the development and improvement of the work. To empower and involve everyone starts with understanding that people have an unlimited potential to grow when they are put in the right environment and inspired by the right purpose. It requires the design of systems that ensure that people can engage every day, and it requires a philosophy of leadership that puts people before profit. Finally, making the commitment to empower and involve everyone requires a leap of faith and an unwavering belief that both the individual and the organization will win in the long term through employing this approach.

A LEARNING ORGANIZATION

The knowledge of an organization is the cumulative knowledge of its people. To have a "learning organization," cumulative knowledge increases over time. As people solve problems, they discover better ways to do things and should share them across the organization. At that point, standard work must be adjusted accordingly.[†]

At its core, continuous improvement requires a commitment to learning. In the absence of learning, organizations are doomed to repeat current practices, relive past problems, and relegate themselves to average results. To successfully develop a culture of continuous improvement, the organization and its leaders must commit to creating an environment that is rich in opportunities to grow and committed to open and honest reflection. Creating an organization committed to continuous learning

---

[*] Shingo Institute, *The Shingo Model*, 20.
[†] Ibid., 21.

takes (1) challenging goals to create gaps and the need for learning, (2) a system in place to ensure that people can easily and effectively contribute to continuous improvement, (3) a method of systematically reflecting on results and improvement efforts to embed the learning, and (4) a process to share learnings and leverage best practices.

PASSION LEADS TO PERFORMANCE

When designed and managed well, culture is a primary driver of sustained business results. The principles of respect and humility found in the Culture Enablers dimension of the *Shingo Model* are much more than just "nice to have" soft skills that leaders need to demonstrate in order to satisfy their employees. Respecting Every Individual and Leading with Humility are key to achieving industry-leading results. Rather than being thought of as a "leadership style," assuring a safe environment, developing people, empowering and engaging everyone, and creating a learning organization must take its rightful place in the organization's strategy. Do this and your organization will become what you aspire it to be.

3

Respect Every Individual

Proposals for improvement that come out of the shop must be evaluated. Some of value waiters, however, spend most of their time pointing out shortcomings in the proposals they see. They go over one proposal after another and reject them, saying, "No good. No good. We've seen this before." I call committee members of this sort improvement assassins. People in the shop will rapidly lose interest in making suggestions if their proposals are killed off so readily. They will either start to think all their suggestions are bad ones or question their own abilities, and eventually they will stop making any suggestions at all.*

—Shigeo Shingo

In the previous chapter, we introduced the Cultural Enablers dimension and broke down the dimension into its two fundamental principles and three supporting concepts. Both principles, Respect Every Individual and Lead with Humility, inform ideal behaviors to create a culture where people are inspired and engaged to participate in creating value for their customers and contributing to the success of their fellow employees. By creating a culture where safety, trust, empowerment, development, and learning are a priority, every organization can maximize engagement and achieve superior business results.

To understand how to achieve these outcomes, let's take a deeper look at the principle of Respect Every Individual. To do this, we will look at the definition of the principle, the meaning of respect, how the Shingo Institute categorizes respect into behavioral benchmarks, and provide

---

* Shigeo Shingo, *The Sayings of Shigeo Shingo: Key Strategies for Plant Improvement*, trans. Andrew P. Dillon (Cambridge, MA: Productivity Press, 1987), 41.

DOI: 10.4324/9781003425519-3

examples of ideal behaviors that organizations are striving to achieve. Finally, we will end the chapter with a case study of AbbVie and one of its leaders, Joseph Kumor. A review of Kumor's view on the principle and a look at AbbVie's systems will illustrate how this organization can embody respect in all they do, as well as the business benefit from implementing respect as a foundational principle.

UNDERSTANDING THE PRINCIPLE

To understand the principle of respect, it is important to refer to the Shingo definition introduced in the last chapter. The Shingo Institute often refers to the definitions it provides as the "business case" for each principle. Think of the business case as the "why" behind the reason for choosing to implement the principle.

The Shingo Institute discusses respect in the following way: *When people feel respected, they give not only their hands but also their minds and their hearts.* Respect for every individual is manifested when an organization structures itself to value each individual as a person and nourish their potential.[†]

As seen in this definition, we start with the acknowledgment that each person has value, and it is our responsibility as an organization and as individual leaders to help nourish their potential. This commitment extends to all employees, customers, suppliers, and society in general. People want respect and they respond to the respect they are shown. It is not only a key driver of engagement, but it also contributes to the overall productivity of an organization. The higher the level of demonstrated respect, the more productive its people are in all they do.

To help our understanding of the definition of this principle, the Shingo Institute also provides a fundamental truth. This fundamental truth is deeper than the definition and helps change the way we think about respect and how we think about what it means to demonstrate respect in

---

[*] Shingo Institute, *The Shingo Model*, 17.
[†] Shingo Institute, "CULTURAL ENABLERS Workshop, version 5.0" (Powerpoint presentation, last modified November 14, 2019), slide 36.

our daily lives. It provides evidence for why principles are universal and helps better inform ideal behavior to which we can align systems.

The Shingo Institute's fundamental truth regarding respect is: *Everyone has value and untapped potential.*

Like the definition of Respect Every Individual, the fundamental truth focuses our attention on the concepts of value and potential. In essence, the statement represents the reason we willingly choose to develop a culture of respect. Because everyone has value and untapped potential, we commit to respecting every individual.

It is important that everyone in the organization understands and actually believes the definition of the principle as well as the fundamental truth. Without this belief, an organization cannot internalize the principle (or identify and understand the ideal behavior it informs), and internalizing the principle is the first step in designing and building systems that drive behavior in an organization.

OWED AND EARNED RESPECT

But what, exactly, is respect? It is a word that gets thrown around in different contexts and can mean a plethora of different things to different people. Since our goal is to create a culture of continuous improvement that is characterized by high levels of engagement and sustainable business results, it is important to understand the principle of respect in this context.

To better understand respect as a concept and principle of operational excellence, it is helpful to separate the two types of respect that leaders must show their people. The first type of respect is *owed* respect. This is the respect that most people reference when asked to describe a culture of respect. Owed respect represents the way people are treated. Owed respect implies that each of us is owed a basic level of civility, with a basic regard for us as individuals that is professional and decent. This is the type of respect that we all believe we deserve regardless of the work we do, our position in the company, our tenure, or our past successes. Providing people with owed respect is important in that when they receive it, it helps them feel a part of the organizational community. When we express owed respect, people feel accepted for who they are. This is critical because feeling accepted for who they are leads people to feel safe, allowing them to be vulnerable and letting them try things and be creative. For example, when we discuss the importance of assuring a safe environment, we are not committing to safety because our people have done something to deserve it. We owe them a safe environment because it is a fundamental sign of decency and civility and because we believe that everyone deserves to be and feel safe. A focus on developing people is also a form of owed respect. In this context, a leader who demonstrates respect for every individual places the development of all people as a strategic focus because this is a basic requirement for creating a professional environment.

The second type of respect is *earned* respect. Earned respect is a respect that is demonstrated when it recognizes the valued achievements or attributes of the particular person. Encouraging earned respect gives people the chance to be unique and to stand out in a positive way. In addition, promoting earned respect is the role of the recognition system as well as encouraged as part of the standard work of leaders in gemba and as part of one-on-one coaching. Unlike owed respect, earned respect is much more about the status a person achieves relative to the behaviors and performance they demonstrate. In this sense, when we empower and engage everyone in continuous improvement activities, we are creating an environment where each individual has the opportunity to earn respect through their hard work and contribution. They also earn respect through the impact they have on the customers and the performance improvements they achieve for the organization. Similarly, the work we do to create a learning environment (embracing opportunities to grow, reflecting on progress, sharing best practices) can be recognized as positive behaviors aligned to the values of the organization and the vision we have for the future. Finally, while a leader plants the seeds for owed and earned respect, they are more responsible for creating the opportunities and systems to achieve and recognize earned respect. It is the team members who bring owed respect to life. Both types of respect should be balanced in the organization for the principle of Respect Every Individual to be mature in an organization's culture.

One last word on creating an environment of respect. Demonstrating respect doesn't mean making things easy. All too often leaders mistakenly believe that creating a culture of respect equates to eliminating sources of stress, removing pain points, and making the job easier. While it is true that a major focus of continuous improvement activities is to improve the working lives of our people, the primary benefit of continuous improvement is the opportunity for people to be challenged to accomplish things they didn't think possible and to take pride in knowing they made a meaningful contribution to the organization. An old sensei used to tell us that if we were not challenging our people and pushing them to excel, then we lacked respect for them as individuals and for their potential to grow. If we truly respected them, we would believe in their ability to take on a challenge and overcome it through struggle and perseverance.

BEHAVIORAL BENCHMARKS

Behavioral benchmarks are large groups of behaviors that are used to break down each principle into groups that are manageable. They can be further broken down into ideal behaviors, the systems that drive them, and Key Behavioral Indicators (KBIs)—what we measure to indicate whether or not we are moving toward ideal behavior. Knowing the ideal behaviors and KBIs helps identify system design parameters and tools that might help enable the system.

As with each principle contained in the *Shingo Model*, the Shingo Institute defines three categories of behavioral benchmarks to help guide us in understanding the principle, but more importantly, in translating the principle into specific and measurable behaviors.

1. **Support:** The behavioral benchmark of support includes all of the behaviors that are involved in investing in others' development and encouraging them to reach their potential. Investing in others may manifest itself in leaders and team members as they commit their time and energy to helping each other develop their skills and grow in their abilities and confidence. Further, support may be demonstrated in the organization's insistence on making formal development opportunities a priority. This can show up not only in how prominent development is in the organization's strategy, but also in how development activities are embedded in the standard work of leaders.

   Regardless of the methods actually chosen to encourage and realize development in the workplace, the principle of respect is embodied when each person in the organization makes development a priority and commits to supporting each other in their development activities.

2. **Recognition:** The second benchmark is recognition. This includes all of the behaviors involved with acknowledging and recognizing the contributions of every employee in the organization. Like development, the key to successfully creating an environment of respect through recognition is to ensure that the contribution of every individual is being recognized, regardless of how big or small the contribution may be. In addition, a culture committed to recognition understands that while it is important for leaders and managers to recognize team members, peer-to-peer recognition is even more powerful. Recognition also includes those behaviors demonstrated by the organization and its leaders as they value the opinions, suggestions, and efforts given by every person, every day.

3. **Community:** The final behavioral benchmark is community. Community includes all of the behaviors demonstrated by leaders, managers, and team members to ensure a physically and emotionally safe workplace for employees. It also includes those actions taken by the organization to ensure that there is not only a strong focus on safety but also a commitment in terms of systems and resources to ensure that focus on safety translates into a safe environment. Demonstrating safety manifests itself when every person in the organization immediately addresses any current or potential safety issues. In addition, the behavioral benchmark of community also includes any and all behaviors that are aligned to minimizing any negative impact the organization, its products, or its processes may have on the environment. It includes the behaviors to ensure that we are good stewards of the environment.

EXAMPLES OF IDEAL BEHAVIORS

Now let's take the behavioral benchmarks and break them down further into ideal behaviors. Ideal behaviors represent those examples of behaviors where leaders, managers, and team members are truly living the principle of respect and supporting each other's growth and development, recognizing the contribution each person makes, and creating a safe environment. It is important to keep in mind that the Shingo Institute has not set in stone a list of ideal behaviors. Rather, ideal behaviors are an evolving set of best practices that align to the *Shingo Model* and that successfully demonstrate the principle and have been tailored to the vision and cultural goals of the organization.

That being said, after helping organizations build world-class cultures for more than 20 years, we have discovered a core set of ideal behaviors that each organization should use as bedrock when defining their culture and assessing its maturity.*

1. **Every person in the company has a personal development plan and co-creates the goals and action plans, which are reviewed on a regular basis.** As Shingo examiners, we would expect to see that the development plans are living documents that are reviewed and updated following each formal conversation between a manager and team member. They should be accessible not only to the managers but also to the team members. When asked to see an example of their development plan, we would expect to see everyone in the organization able to access their development plan easily, be well versed in both the content of the plan and the status of each action, and passionately tell us why they have chosen their particular development goals and what accomplishing the goals will mean to them.

2. **One-on-one coaching follows a consistent process and is evident at all levels of the organization.** The companies that are most successful at building effective coaching systems have typically invested in providing appropriate coaching, training, and support for all people. These managers are actively encouraged to seek out and maximize opportunities to coach individual team members and teams, including tier meetings/huddles, one-on-ones, and gemba visits. The impact of this coaching is evident in the increasing competence and confidence of those being coached, who frequently become effective coaches.

---

* It is important to reiterate that the purpose of this book is not to create a laundry list of every behavioral example we have seen. A key to your success in creating a culture of respect and humility is your ability to focus on the critical few behaviors that will lead to the outcomes you are looking for. While there are arguably many more behaviors exhibited in a mature organization than the five behaviors we have included here, these five behaviors represent a starting point from which to build. If you successfully embed each one of them, you will be further along in your maturity than 80 percent of the organizations we meet.

3. **There is a formal process for recognition that is frequent, timely, specific, and visual.** In the most mature organizations, the focus of recognition is primarily on the expressed appreciation of the individual and their inherent value, rather than on reward. A great system of recognition is both visual and visible and includes both manager-to-team member and peer-to-peer recognition. There is active monitoring of the system to ensure that it is fair and equitable and encourages participation across the entire enterprise. The process has been documented as a part of standard work for leaders and team members, and when asked, employees can tell you how the process works, the last time they were recognized, and the topic of recognition.

4. **All employees participate in a consistent and closed-loop suggestion system.** The suggestion system is typically simple, visual, and accessible to all employees. There is a process in place for tracking participation of teams and team members across the organization, and contributions are both formally and informally recognized by managers. Also, employees actively participate in the recognition system through team-based problem-solving during huddles, and improvement events and the focus of the system are on implementing ideas and ensuring that improvements have been made.

5. **Near misses are captured, escalated, and addressed immediately.** In world-class organizations where safety is always front and center, there is a robust and proactive approach to safety with all employees, including team members, who are encouraged to actively participate in identifying and reporting hazards and near misses. The system to support this is accessible to all employees, and there is a rapid follow-up to all reports logged. The proactive nature of the system, which is focused on the elimination of potential sources of future problems, is overt. And, finally, the organization is invested in creating a culture where everyone views safety as a personal commitment.

As you can see from these five ideal behaviors, each one relates to the larger behavioral benchmarks of support, recognition, and safety. In addition, when you review each behavior, you start to see the connection to the systems that will directly support the development of the ideal behavior and its sustainment over time. Finally, while we have not explicitly defined each behavior with respect to how leaders, managers, and team members exhibit the behavior on a daily basis, it becomes clear that for a behavior to be ideal, it must be expressed in ways that help every person in the organization know how the behavior manifests itself in a mature culture and what their role is in bringing the behavior to life.

PRINCIPLES IN ACTION: RESPECT AT ABBVIE

In 2011, Abbott Laboratories announced that it was splitting into two healthcare companies. One was to be a diversified medical products company, Abbott, and the other would be a new researched-based global biopharmaceutical company, AbbVie. Today, AbbVie employs 48,000 people in more than 70 countries. The split allowed AbbVie to create a new culture with an already established workforce and product set. Since that time, AbbVie has become a cultural benchmark, winning national best workplace awards in 21 countries.

The Ballytivnan site in Sligo, Ireland, was founded in 1974 as an Abbott Nutrition facility. Ballytivnan currently produces 7+ million auto-injector pens for a very significant company product used to treat a range of autoimmune conditions, including rheumatoid arthritis, Crohn's disease, psoriasis, and other immune-mediated inflammatory conditions. Owing to the continued success of AbbVie Ballytivnan, the site has been selected as the site of choice to manufacture AbbVie's new drug delivery devices for advanced-stage Parkinson's disease, increasing output to 8+ million devices per year.

THE LEAN JOURNEY AT ABBVIE, BALLYTIVNAN

Joseph Kumor, senior director of Environmental Health Safety at AbbVie Ballytivnan, says,

> In April 2014, I was appointed site director at the AbbVie site in Sligo, Ireland. Prior to that, I had various business excellence and continuous improvement leadership roles. I had been aware of the *Shingo Model* for some time, and when Eilish Henry came to Sligo to talk to me about it and

the *Shingo Guiding Principles*, I was reminded how powerfully they reso-nated with my own leadership philosophy and approach.

Together with his leadership team at the Sligo site, Kumor becomes resolute in his commitment that the site adopts best practices in Lean manufacturing principles in both designing the site and building a culture of respect and engagement.

SHAPING THE CULTURE THROUGH IDEAL BEHAVIORS

"At AbbVie, we embody our working culture through a core set of behaviors for all employees at all levels," says Kumor.

> The behaviors are grounded in the principles of respect and humility and make it clear that how we achieve results is equally as important as achiev-ing them. Our behaviors are strongly aligned with the *Shingo Model* and, as such, our ideal behaviors reflect and reinforce our desired culture.

The AbbVie Ballytivnan behaviors have evolved over time as the organization has matured and learned. Following is the most recent version of them:

All for One AbbVie

- Operate with an enterprise perspective, putting overall AbbVie before individual or functional interests.
- Inspire and motivate others toward a shared purpose.
- Influence colleagues to achieve cross-functional alignment.
- Manage inclusivity and equity across all.

Decide Smart and Sure

- Deal comfortably with risk and ambiguity, and change course when needed.
- Know the business and the cross-functional contributions needed to deliver results.

- Make timely, high-quality decisions with less-than-perfect information.
- Live AbbVie values and act consistently with our ethics, obligations, and the law.

Agile and Accountable

- Set clear strategic and robust implementation plans.
- Give full accountability when delegating; accept full accountability when delegating to others.
- Deliver business results while positioning AbbVie for long-term success.
- Simplify how work gets done and remove unnecessary bureaucracy.

Clear and Courageous

- Act respectfully yet courageously and say what needs to be said.
- Manage conflict and difficult conversations in a constructive, transparent way.
- Use mistakes, failures, and reflection as vehicles for learning and improvement.
- Communicate openly and honestly with all colleagues.

Make Possibilities Real

- Look outside AbbVie for new ideas to stimulate innovation.
- Connect unrelated concepts and generate original or unique ideas.
- Create an environment in which people appropriately experiment and challenge the status quo.
- Be persistent and resilient and find a way to move good ideas forward.

THE IMPORTANCE OF SAFETY

"In my view, the clearest indicator of the principle of Respect Every Individual is safety," continues Kumor.

This includes the safety of all our employees, the safety of our product, the safety of our customers and suppliers, and the safety of the wider community and environment in which we operate. This has always been our first key metric on our balanced scorecard, and it's what led me to my current role at AbbVie as senior director of Environmental Health Safety at AbbVie.

In addition to the importance of safety in both the strategy and core metrics, Kumor also focuses on aligning leadership behaviors to ensure that ideal behaviors and commitment to respect through safety are reinforced on a daily basis.

Kumor says,

> I had the key responsibility to set the expectations for managers at all levels and to role model those agreed behaviors. I developed appropriate leader standard work and aimed to adhere to that as robustly as possible and to be held accountable for doing so. This included daily visits to the Gemba to "see reality," to talk with frontline team members, to recognize contributions, and to coach for improvement.
>
> I am a passionate advocate for leaders/managers as coaches and we invested significantly in developing our coaching system at the site. I needed to lead by example for the organization. I held formal one-on-ones with every employee on site minimally one time per year. It gave me an opportunity to get to know each employee on a personal level, providing them direct coaching, feedback, and assisting to set the framework for their personal and professional development plans. It also provided an opportunity to understand each functional area's strengths and opportunities, thus giving more direct feedback on where we as a leadership team would develop action plans to address those opportunities directly from the feedback of our employees.
>
> No matter what level of the organization you worked, every voice was equally important, and everyone was heard. This then enabled our senior management team and all our other people leaders to do the same within their functional organization by hearing the voice of their employees and creating action plans to consistently address all areas for improvement in our organization. These actions aligned with AbbVie's culture which aligned with the *Shingo Model* and helped ensure we demonstrated through our commitment to safety, our empowerment of our people and our coaching system that we aligned with the principle of Respect Every Individual.

RESULTS

Owing to the dedication and performance of the team, the site transformed from a backup molding facility to a Center of Excellence for drug delivery devices. The following are some of the results the site was able to achieve by transforming its culture and embedding the principles of respect in their system and leadership behaviors.

- The site's culture and systems enabled rapid growth, including five product launches and five ISO certifications.
- AbbVie Ballytivnan was one of the first companies in Ireland to receive the European Sustainable Asset Management Certification.
- The site was recognized two years in a row (2016 and 2017) as a Great Place to Work by *Fortune.*
- In 2018, the site was awarded the Shingo Prize for Operational Excellence, a mere five years after it first came into existence. This is an extraordinary achievement and ranks as one of the most ambitious excellence journeys of any Shingo Prize recipient. Typically, the recipients have been on their Lean/operational excellence journey for 10 or more years.

Kumor summarizes, "Our people are our greatest asset, and we are proud of our culture. Our culture is a result of the dedication, hard work, and pride of our employees to make an impact on the lives of patients around the world."

PAY ATTENTION AND CELEBRATE ACCOMPLISHMENTS

"I have a foundational belief that business results start with culture and your people," says Doug Conant, former CEO of Campbell Soup. "Over the years, I've worked on acknowledging others for their efforts. I've managed to marry tough-minded performance standards with tender heartedness. Believe it or not, I have sent roughly 30,000 handwritten notes to employees over the last decade, from maintenance people to senior executives. I let them know that I am personally paying attention and celebrating their accomplishments. It's the least you can do for people who do things to help your company and industry. On the face of it, writing handwritten notes may seem like a waste of time. But in my experience, they build goodwill and lead to higher productivity."*

---

* Douglas R. Conant, "Secrets of Positive Feedback," *Harvard Business Review,* February 16, 2011.

4

Lead with Humility

People will not be set in motion until they are convinced on an emotional level based on trust—until they can say, "That's right! I know that'll make the job easier and improve quality at the same time!" or "It looks kind of hard, but I believe the guy who's telling me this, so it's got to work!" [*]

—*Shigeo Shingo*

The second of the *Shingo Guiding Principles* is Lead with Humility. As indicated in the principle itself, the focus of the principle is leadership. Like respect, humility contributes to creating a culture that assures the safety of everyone, engages each person to their fullest, develops the skills and abilities of their people, and continuously learns through improvement, reflection, and best practice sharing.

UNDERSTANDING THE PRINCIPLE

As we did with Respect Every Individual, we will start our exploration of the principle of humility with the definition provided by the Shingo Institute. The definition of the principles provides us with much-needed context and helps us understand the outcomes we are striving for and the effects our behaviors have on those we lead.

The Shingo Institute discusses humility in the following way: *Organizational and personal growth is enabled when leaders work to bring*

---

[*] Shigeo Shingo, *Sayings of Shigeo Shingo: Key Strategies for Plant Improvement,* trans. Andrew P. Dillon (Cambridge, MA: Productivity Press, 1987), 130.

DOI: 10.4324/9781003425519-4

*out the best in those they lead. They seek out and value the ideas of others, and they are willing to change when they learn something new. Leaders trust others to make good decisions.**

The definition of Leading with Humility puts a leader's role in the organization and the outcomes we seek to achieve culturally at the forefront. When humility is what we seek, our expressed goal for leaders is to achieve growth—growth in the organization and growth in the individuals working in the organization. This can only be enabled when leaders willingly adopt an approach steeped in the characteristics and behaviors of humility and focused on trusting and engaging others. When leaders are willing to trust others and focus on their own weaknesses, culture transparency and continuous learning can be established. When transparency and learning characterize your culture, then daily innovation and risk-taking become routine.

The definition also sheds light on the importance of leaders embracing change and being open to learning. This commitment to challenging ourselves to grow as leaders is a central theme in leading from a position of humility. It is not enough for leaders to trust their people and be open to their ideas. Great leaders are also relentless in their self-reflection and commitment to improving their skills as a leader and their effectiveness in getting results through their people. The concept of growth and self-improvement forms the basis of the Shingo Institute's fundamental truth.

The Shingo Institute's fundamental truth regarding humility is: *All growth requires vulnerability.*

The fundamental truth for this principle is short and sweet and focuses our attention on two key concepts: Growth and vulnerability. In addition, it forces us to acknowledge that vulnerability is more than a mere quality of a humble leader. In fact, to accomplish our goals of organizational and personal growth, vulnerability is a prerequisite. Vulnerability in this context is the willingness to allow others to guide change in the organization. It is the vulnerability to admit that we don't have all the answers and to acknowledge that if we engage the hearts and minds of everyone to give their improvement ideas, the final solution will be better than we could have imagined, and the organization will be stronger because of it. Vulnerability requires leaders to give their people power over things that can and do influence a leader's performance. When

---

* Shingo Institute, "CULTURAL ENABLERS Workshop, version 5.0" (Powerpoint presentation, last modified November 14, 2019), slide 76.

leaders choose to put themselves in a vulnerable and transparent position, decision-making becomes more decentralized and devolves to lower levels in the organization.

While putting oneself in a vulnerable position is the goal, there are core components of humility (or being a humble leader) that must be in place. These components represent the mindset leaders need to adopt in order to see the power of vulnerability in the workplace and to model the behaviors characterized by humble leaders.

1. **Understanding Yourself:** To understand yourself as an individual and a leader, it is critical to develop self-awareness of your strengths and your weaknesses. Being clear about both strengths and weaknesses is a critical component of developing humility. It is this self-awareness that humble leaders aspire to develop, but also strive to maintain through regular reflection.

2. **Relating to Others:** The second core component of humility is how leaders relate to others. Seeing yourself in terms of your relationship with others and how others perceive you provides a window into your effectiveness as a leader and your opportunities to grow. Recognizing these relationship gaps contributes to being vulnerable and open to growth. Relating to others also encompasses the need to be as concerned about the welfare of others as you are about your own welfare. Without concern for others' welfare, leaders do not have the ability to see themselves in the context of how others see them. In order to truly consider the perspective of others, I must first care as much about their perspective as I do my own.

3. **Finding Perspective:** Finally, how you experience life events and your relationship to them requires a unique perspective if humility is to be present. Leading with humility requires you to view the actions you take as a leader and the experiences you have with your people in relation to a greater whole. The purpose you see in your desired results and behaviors must align to a larger purpose that places the welfare of others first and focus on passion before performance.

If understanding yourself, relating to others, and having the right perspective are critical components to achieving humility in thought and action, then it may be useful to think of these core components as precursors to our ability to demonstrate humility in how we lead our people. Remember, our goal is not so much to understand what humility means, but rather to understand at a behavioral level what it looks like when humility is embedded in our approach to leading people.

To understand what it means to lead with humility, it is helpful to also look at the characteristics and behaviors exhibited by humble leaders. These characteristics and behaviors have been well documented in the research and business literature on the nature of humility and more importantly, what defines humility as a leadership style.

First, humble leaders are typically more aware of their speech and behavior. They are not only purposeful in what they say and how they act, but they reflect on the impact of both speech and behavior on the attitudes, perceptions, and behaviors of others. This leads them to be more in tune with their employees. Being in tune with their employees is also manifested in how they relate to others and the quality of relationships they build with their people.

Next, humble leaders tend to have a better understanding of the bigger picture (or vision) of the organization. They strive to see that their actions as leaders directly reflect the quality of life their people experience on a daily basis and that this quality of life translates into organizational performance. This focus on understanding the bigger picture translates into leaders having a better or more objective idea of how their actions are contributing to the realization of the vision. Understanding and appreciating the impact we have as leaders is a characteristic of humility.

Another characteristic of humble leaders is that they tend to be more focused on leading for the common good. Leading for the common good and being aware of the bigger picture go hand in hand and speak to a leader's desire to help maximize the welfare of others and view the needs of the whole before the needs of self. That is not to say that humble leaders don't also focus time and energy on their own goals and needs. Leading for the common good merely means that leaders understand the old adage, "you can get everything in life you want if you just help enough other people get what they want."

Humble leaders also tend to be more connected to their people. This deep connection shows itself in a variety of ways. First, they recognize the extent to which their team members understand and support organizational goals. They spend time ensuring that everyone knows the "why" behind the goals and the work to be done and they commit to regular and impactful communication and coaching to ensure that team members are aligned.

Second, humble leaders understand what their team members want and need from them as leaders and from each of their peers to be successful. They are keenly aware of what motivates each of their team members on an individual basis, and they help impact the ability of each individual to accomplish their personal and professional goals. Finally, humble leaders understand that the needs of their people can change over time based on the nature of the work, their shared experiences, and their development.

Before we move to the behavioral benchmarks for the principle Lead with Humility, it is important to note that the characteristics and qualities of a humble leader are not defined by the size of organization, geographic location, or cultural context. A Catalyst study surveyed more than 1,500 workers from Australia, China, Germany, India, Mexico, and the United States.* The study identified key behaviors of successful leaders. The results of the study mirror our discussion of the characteristics of humble leaders. First, successful leaders empower their people to learn and develop. Second, successful leaders demonstrate acts of personal humility, such as learning from criticism and admitting mistakes. Next, successful leaders display acts of courage, such as taking personal risks for the greater good. Finally, successful leaders are strong as they hold people responsible for their results.

BEHAVIORAL BENCHMARKS

The Shingo Institute defines three categories of behavioral benchmarks to help guide us in understanding the principle Lead with Humility. The behavioral benchmarks also help us in our work to translate the principle into specific and measurable behaviors.

1. **Servant Leadership:** The first behavioral benchmark is servant leadership. Servant leadership includes all those behaviors the leaders exhibit that demonstrate the consideration of others first. A key illustration of servant leadership is the work leaders do to remove barriers that prevent team members from being successful in their

---

* Jeanine Prime and Elizabeth R. Salib, *Inclusive Leadership: The View From Six Countries* (Catalyst, 2014).

daily work and/or prevent them from developing their full potential. These barriers may manifest themselves in a lack of time or resources or a lack of skill or confidence for the task at hand. In any event, a leader's job is to remove barriers and clear a path for each of their team members to succeed.

2. **Courage:** The second benchmark is courage. Courage includes all those behaviors that enable leaders and team members to recognize strengths and weaknesses, acknowledge mistakes, and learn from all relevant people and resources, whether those resources are internal or external to the organization. Leaders create an environment where mistakes, errors, and defects are quickly made visible and are viewed as opportunities to improve. Leaders encourage their teams to learn from each other as well as from other teams. Leaders provide the time, resources, and opportunities for teams to learn from other sources that are not directly related to work. Finally, in their work to create a learning organization, leaders encourage their people to actively seek feedback in order to improve. Leaders model this behavior through the feedback they seek both from their managers and from team members.

3. **Empowerment:** The final benchmark of Lead with Humility is empowerment. Empowerment includes all those behaviors that enable decision-making to be devolved to the lowest appropriate level. Empowerment also includes those behaviors that demonstrate the trust we place in others and how we support each other's growth and success on a daily basis. The organization and its leaders play a critical role in empowerment insofar as they work together to equip their people with the necessary information, materials, processes, and resources to make relevant decisions. In addition, leaders must strive to maintain a reasonable balance between forgiving honest mistakes and holding people accountable for their decisions.

EXAMPLES OF IDEAL BEHAVIORS

Now that we have explored the behavioral benchmarks of Lead with Humility, it is time to break those benchmarks down into ideal behaviors. As we have done with Respect Every Individual, these ideal behaviors are merely a selection we have chosen to illustrate how you as a leader can begin to see what humility can mean to your daily life and what the presence of humility in a mature organization looks like.

1. **Leaders ensure that adequate time is provided for development activities.** The best companies view development as an investment in their future and can point to significant business benefits they have derived from providing time for people development. The time spent in development can be formal training of new skills and capabilities, or it can be the time devoted to allowing people to solve problems and work as a team to improve performance. Regardless of the form it takes, it is of prime importance that leaders are formally scheduling time for development and following up to ensure that the development activities are meaningful to the people involved.

2. **Resources are provided based on alignment to strategic goals, a structured process, and timely feedback to all requests.** In world-class organizations, we seldom see any evidence of resources being allocated to "vanity projects." Rather, there are robust processes for prioritizing resource allocation to strategically important projects. If there is contention for resources, leaders will have mature and informed discussions that involve all the stakeholders and will seek an agreed outcome. The importance of allocating resources based on strategic priority and ensuring inclusive dialogue and timely feedback is what characterizes these behaviors as contributing to a humble approach to leadership.

3. **There is a process to share ideas from other areas, which is implemented on a regular basis.** The most successful organizations have highly effective knowledge-sharing systems to ensure that learning from one area is shared in a timely manner with all other areas, and that this shared learning is leveraged to benefit the whole enterprise. These organizations also typically have daily kaizen (continuous improvement) systems that provide a high level of visibility across the organization with respect to the ideas generated, approved, and implemented. This best practice sharing of ideas serves to contribute to developing a learning organization and also acts as a method of recognition. This includes recognition by leaders that great ideas can come from anywhere at any time as well as recognition of the individuals who have successfully improved performance through continuous improvement activities.

4. **Feedback is regularly solicited and reviewed in all areas.** In mature organizations, we often see formal processes for seeking 360-degree feedback, which is used to shape the development plans of both individual team members and leaders. In these companies, there is often also a formal system for tracking levels of people engagement with regular employee surveys and follow-up plans. In addition, there are systems in place for ensuring that leaders at all levels are regularly in the gemba, meeting team members and listening to their concerns, suggestions, and achievements. This time in the gemba—in addition to a system of tiered huddles—allows for open and honest dialogue. It also provides leaders with an opportunity to view their leadership effectiveness from the perspective of the relationships they form and the interactions they have.

5. **Decision-making is devolved to the lowest appropriate level with feedback provided on decisions that are made.** These behaviors are most commonly seen from two perspectives. First, it is seen in how much autonomy leaders give to teams to self-direct closed-loop problem-solving. This indicates the level of trust the leader has in his or her team and the level of vulnerability the leader shows in their actions. The more decision-making that is entrusted to the team, the higher the engagement and the more the trust placed on the team. Second, the very best companies typically have robust and mature tiered huddle structures that support rapid response to issues and devolved decision-making. When issues do need to be escalated to a higher tier or level, there is immediate action taken and feedback given regarding the decision made, the action to be taken, and the responsible party. This process of first trusting people to make decisions and then using the tiered huddles to ensure rapid follow-up leads to confidence in the effectiveness of the system and a feeling of being valued on the part of the team members.

PRINCIPLES IN ACTION: HUMILITY AT ABBOTT NUTRITION ONE CHINA

Abbott broke ground at the Jiaxing plant in 2011. It was Abbott's biggest investment in China, and a corporate strategy was deployed in 2012 to establish a One China Supply Chain Enterprise. One China's mission is to deliver the highest quality nutrition products to help improve their customers' quality of life. The One China model integrates the entire supply chain from end to end, incorporating the true source of farming, purchasing, planning, supplier relationship management, manufacturing, commercial quality assurance, distribution, and e-commerce. The site boasts approximately 300 employees and provides science-based nutrition products to people at every stage of life, enabling them to live life to the fullest by providing products like Similac, Eleva, Ensure, Glucerna, and PediaSure.

Fanny Chen was appointed the senior leader for Abbott One China in 2011, initially as managing director of China Supply Chain and Operations Development. She had previously held senior leadership roles within the wider Abbott organization. Her responsibilities in the One China role included building the supply chain organization in China with two manufacturing plants and five regional distribution centers. She was also responsible for overseeing the construction and start-up of the greenfield manufacturing plant with over a $300 million investment and developing the China dairy strategy to support $900 million in annual sales with more than 100 stock keeping units (SKUs). A key focus for Chen was building the talent pool for the China operations while coaching, mentoring, and inspiring China local senior leaders to merge Abbott culture with the Chinese environment in mind. At the same time, she was effectively managing local, provincial, and central government relationships.

In 2016, Chen was appointed divisional vice president of Greater China Supply Chain and Strategic Relations. The challenge and opportunity that Chen and her leadership team faced were building an organizational culture that was based on the concepts of business excellence, which is so important to Abbott, as well as Abbott's Pledge Behaviors and the principles of humility and respect, while also fully reflecting China's local, regional, and national cultures and phenomenal history.

THE LEAN JOURNEY AT ABBOTT ONE CHINA

The site formally began its Lean journey with the introduction of its operational excellence model in 2013. This model focuses on the foundational pillars of people and culture. It also beautifully blends an approach that is both top-down and bottom-up. The element of the model that is top-down is creating and cascading strategy from senior leadership to daily operations. The bottom-up elements are the commitment to daily management and continuous improvement in all areas.

A key element of the site's excellence model is its focus on behaviors. The site has adopted Abbott's "Our Pledge Behaviors, Our Foundation" and ensures that each person at One China understands and seeks to model these behaviors in all they do. Following is Abbott's "Our Pledge Behaviors, Our Foundation."

Our Pledge Behaviors, Our Foundation

One Team, One Voice, One Goal: We take initiative and help others when the need arises. Everyone is committed to teamwork and cross-functional collaboration. Everyone understands their role in achieving the Supply Chain strategy.

I Am Accountable: Everyone clearly understands what is expected of them and holds themselves accountable for the quality of their work. We make commitments and will deliver on them.

I Am a Leader: In our team, managers are not the only leaders. Each individual contributor takes opportunities to learn and grow and becomes a leader in their own right. When new tasks arise, we are open to taking them on. We are encouraged to ask tough questions to drive open and transparent dialogue.

I Drive Continuous Improvement: Cross-function and cross-level, we listen to others' opinions and ideas. We are encouraged to challenge routine work by thinking of ideas in new ways. We don't settle for surface-level understanding, we aim to discover the root cause and take the necessary action.

I Make Timely, Fact-Based Decisions: Before jumping to a conclusion, we consult all available resources, materials, equipment, and information. Decisions are made on facts and data instead of gut-feel.

My Work Matters: All employees understand the importance of everyone's job. We are proud to work for nutrition because what we do impacts the lives of our consumers. And we are confident that we are doing our job right.

These behaviors, along with their systems, help create a culture of respect and humility at Abbott One China. They also align each person to the organization's vision to "unleash human potential through the power of scientific-based nutrition."

"Our Pledge Behaviors have not just become a theme of the year, it is our everyday job, everyday life," says Chen. "It helps guide us in our daily actions as a uniting standard helping communicate why we and what we do every day is so important."

In 2014, the site introduced 14 work streams to identify and eliminate waste through value stream mapping, kaizen events, and the idea program. In 2015, Abbott One China kicked off the belt program by certifying 24 Green Belts and 80 Yellow Belts. Since 2017, the site has redefined the operational excellence model and developed an enterprise excellence model. This model places emphasis on the 4Ps—people, process, purpose, and performance—to continuously drive the improvement culture and deliver sustainable growth.

SHAPING CULTURE BY LEADING WITH HUMILITY

At Abbott One China, leadership understands that people are the indispensable foundation of all their operations and leader actions reflect the goal of creating a supportive working environment that incorporates individual needs and world views, as well as aligns with the One China Mission to "build a high-quality organization to deliver the highest quality products to improve people's quality of life." The culture, built upon the Pledge Behaviors, was gradually developed to empower employees to achieve both personal and workplace success.

Chen believes that the principle Lead with Humility is most clearly manifest in the behaviors of leaders and managers. She recognizes that at Abbott One China, the wider team comes from a culture of humility, respect for authority, and maintaining harmony. In the workplace, this could result in employees being reluctant to speak up and challenge managers and leaders. To counteract this, she works to build the confidence of her people to respectfully challenge each other, the leaders, and the managers and to share their ideas for improving their work area and processes. Chen effectively uses the Mindful Leader Program to encourage all leaders to be visible and accessible, to be willing to show vulnerability and engage in "contracting" conversations with their team members, and to coach and mentor them for improvement. Chen leads by example and has been a very visible and supportive leader, having developed her leader standard work with frequent gemba walks and maintaining a robust and disciplined adherence to these practices. This has meant frequent travel between the Shanghai offices and the manufacturing plant in Jiaxing, but Chen has willingly undertaken the journeys to ensure that she continues to connect to the wider One China team and is available to them, not just if and when problems arise, but to recognize and celebrate with them their contributions and achievements.

THE IMPORTANCE OF DEVELOPMENT

At Abbott One China, the goal is to give employees a sense of purpose and empowerment as well as to provide opportunities for them to improve their professional skills. Employee development is one of the site's core strategies to help provide focus on every employee's career development. Employees gain the experience of growing together with the company from onboarding and through developing their skills, knowledge, and competency in their careers with Abbott. Under Chen's leadership, the site aims to optimize employee engagement and development through the development of Career Connect, Career Ladder, and Talent Management Review (TMR), as well as the Mindful Leadership program. The Career Ladder program engages employees by providing a clear development roadmap to achieve personal and professional growth and allows the Abbott One China team to improve business productivity and agility.

Employees are also encouraged to develop a career vision map as well as long-term and short-term career plans to help them achieve their career goals. Talent Management Review (TMR) is one of the key development platforms in place to ensure that each critical position is reviewed and well planned with internal pipeline successors. The TMR process is connected to talents through Individual Development Plans, which are developed to equip employees for that role. Finally, leaders are responsible for providing career coaching and mentorship to help align employee career development with business needs. They also support employee development by providing growth opportunities, such as job rotation, job scope expansion, and special project assignment.

Dong Chenghao, a packaging technician at Abbott One China, said,

I joined the Jiaxing plant five years ago, starting as an Operator 1 in the packaging area. Now, I am a Packaging Technician 2, which is my fourth role in Abbott, thanks to the Career Ladder platform. Development on the Career Ladder platform has been a meaningful experience for me. With clear expectations and development plans with my frontline leader's support, I am now able to work more independently. I am glad that a lot of my ideas to optimize the process and eliminate waste have been approved and implemented in the packaging area.

LEADING WITH HUMILITY THROUGH MINDFUL LEADERS

In addition to the work done with employees through Career Connect and the Talent Management Review process, Abbott One China focuses on leadership development to ensure that leaders lead with humility, respect employees in various roles and positions with different educational backgrounds, and provide coaching and mentoring to enable employees to perform at their best. Ultimately, the goal is to develop leaders who are able to engage employees to support business growth and provide an experience so employees feel they are growing together with the company.

To develop its leaders and build stronger employee engagement within the culture, Abbott One China launched the Mindful Leader development program. The site started the journey with its senior leadership team in 2017, and the program has since been cascaded to all leader levels in the organization. The Mindful Leader program enables the site to significantly develop its leadership effectiveness in five behaviors through the four windows of the world.

- By responding effectively and mindfully instead of reacting defensively. This is key to maintaining healthy relationships.
- By integrating the power of vulnerability into the leadership style while also recognizing the vast difference between being vulnerable and being a victim.
- By transforming potential conflict situations into opportunities to collaborate with wider teams.

- By having more impactful courageous conversations and less destructive and ineffective criticizing conversations.
- By developing self-responsible and empowered team members through advanced coaching skills.

These five behaviors help the site to build effective leaders who grow in their roles and empower each team member to challenge themselves and their team mindfully.

The Mindful Leader program is a cultural journey at Abbott One China that every employee is fully aware of and able to use to guide his or her behavior. Leaders make full use of Mindful Leader tools and concepts to become role models of the Shingo principles Lead with Humility and Respect Every Individual.

RESULTS

Due to Abbott One China's relentless commitment to developing their people and driving continuous improvement, the site has experienced tremendous success. Here is a sample of some of its accomplishments:

- Zero Lost Time Accidents from 2012 to 2019
- #2 site for Abbott Environmental Health and Safety (EHS) Plant of the Year in 2016
- Abbott Global EHS Plant of the Year in 2017
- Batch Right First Time (BRFT) improvement from 30 percent in 2014 to 99 percent in 2018
- Nonconformance dropped from 96 percent in 2014 to 18 percent in 2018
- The site received quality and food safety certifications from 2014 to 2019
- The site received six EHS certifications from 2014 to 2019
- The site received LEED Gold green energy certificate in 2016
- Zero Waste to Landfill Plant since 2015. Eighty-three percent of all waste is reused or recycled
- Reduced cycle time by 21 days from 2014 to 2019
- Improved overall equipment effectiveness by 30 percent from 2014 to 2019

Finally, the work done by Chen and her team has led to the development of a world-class culture. Not only did the site receive the Shingo Prize in 2019, but it was also voted as the Top Employer in China and a Great Place to Work for eight consecutive years (from 2012 to 2019).

LISTENING IS CRUCIAL FOR SOUND LEADERSHIP

J.W. "Bill" Marriott Jr., executive chair of Marriott International, said, "The four most important words in the English language are what, do, you, think. Listen to your people and learn." Marriott believes that humility and a willingness to listen to opinions that differ from your own are crucial for sound leadership. He describes how he learned this lesson from an offhand remark made by President Eisenhower while he was staying at his parent's property in the winter of 1954. Unsure whether to go outside to shoot quail that his father had bought for the occasion or to stay inside by the fire, Eisenhower turned to the 22-year-old Marriott and asked, "What do you think I should do?" Marriott recalls being flattered that Eisenhower was even remotely interested in his opinion. "What do you think …" is a simple question, but it sets the best leaders apart and builds trust, respect, and collaboration more than clever answers ever can.[*]

---

[*] Dr. Margi Warrell, "Bill Marriott: Four Things Great Leaders Do Differently," June 25, 2016. linke din.com/pulse/bill-marriott-four-things-great-leaders-do-margie-warrell/.

5

Enabling Culture at TESSEI

We have spent time diving into each principle to understand what it means, how it enables a world-class culture, the key systems needed, and how it looks when your people are living the principle every day. Next, we turn our attention to a case study that helps bring to life the impact an engaging culture can have on your people, the leadership commitment and behaviors necessary to foster this type of culture, and the business results that follow. To illustrate the effects of enabling your culture, we turn our attention to TESSEI.*

A subsidiary of JR East (East Japan Railway Company), TESSEI is the cleaning company responsible for turning around the famous Shinkansen trains (bullet trains) in under seven minutes. Founded in 1952 to clean train cars on the Japanese National Railways, the company cleans more than 2,000 Shinkansen trains per day across four stations: Tokyo, Ueno, Oyama, and Tabata. TESSEI's work represents some of the most complicated cleaning operations in the world and at the time of this writing, the company has become synonymous with the Japanese concept of *omotenashi* (hospitality), winning numerous awards both domestically and internationally. This is in stark contrast to the condition the company was in back in 2005.

At that time, the company was reeling from four years of declining business performance. Revenue was falling an average of 3.1 percent per year, while the volume of trains needing to be cleaned per day had risen by an average of 2.8 percent per year over the same period.† To

---

* This section reprinted with permission from Michael Martyn, *Management for Omotenashi* (Portland, OR: SISU Press, 2022), 46–60.
† All company performance data taken from Ethan Bernstein and Ryan W. Buell, "Trouble at TESSEI," *Harvard Business Review* (October 20, 2015): 1–16. doi: 9-615-044.

DOI: 10.4324/9781003425519-5

further exacerbate the problems, management had employed cost-cutting initiatives to combat the falling revenues, which had led to a dramatic decrease in operational performance. By increasing the percentage of part-time employees from 26 percent to 52 percent, annual turnover reached as high as 54 percent per year, leading to a dramatic increase in operational mistakes as well as customer complaints. To add insult to injury, safety accidents had increased sixfold in the previous four years and there seemed to be no end in sight for abating the issues plaguing the company.

In addition to operational performance issues, TESSEI faced rapidly declining employee morale as well as a significant problem with its brand in the marketplace. At the time, the company was known to be a "last-resort" employer. Most employees had come to work at TESSEI because they did not have anywhere else to go due to their employment histories. Cleaning trains was considered a 3K job: *kitanai* (dirty), *kitsui* (difficult), and *kiken* (dangerous). Customers looked down on TESSEI employees and the employees themselves felt ashamed to work at the company. One employee stated, "My parents do not tell others where their daughter is working as they think working at a cleaning company would look shameful to others. They keep it a secret."*

The condition of management was not much better than that of the employees. Managerial misconduct in the early 2000s had led to a loss of trust and revenue from JR East, to which the response was a significant increase in managerial monitoring and controls. However, while the core cleaning processes had been clearly defined as early as 2001, the tighter management attempted to control the behaviors of the employees in accordance with the standard, the worse the results. Mistakes grew, delays increased, and complaints mounted.

To compound the problem, top management of the company was not aligned, financial accounting practices were sloppy, and there was a severe "us versus them" mentality between leadership and the employees.

One employee described the culture:

> The company has a culture like *taiikukai-kei* (strong command and control culture). If we deviate from what we are supposed to do even a little, senior staff points that out. Senior staff are really scary and intimidating. They are years older than me, so they are exacting. We are scolded and yelled at in

---

* Bernstein and Buell, "Trouble at TESSEI," 7.

the passage even with a minor mistake such as being slow to push a button to rotate chairs or picking up someone's broom. Of course, there are some that are kind, but the overall impression is scary.*

ENTER TERUO YABE

After a 39-year career at JR East, Mr Teruo Yabe (Figure 5.1) was appointed the director and general manager of TESSEI and tasked with leading the turnaround. Yabe came to TESSEI with a strong background in safety and transportation logistics, but he had little in the way of experience with cleaning. Faced with no increase in revenue or resources, Yabe set about transforming the organization with a focus on customer experience, employee engagement, and leadership development. Over

http://ihcsacafe-en.ihcsa.or.jp/news/tessei/

FIGURE 5.1
Teruo Yabe.

---

* Ibid., "Trouble at TESSEI," 7.

the next two years, Yabe would see the dramatic results of his focus on redefining leadership at TESSEI and creating a direct connection between the customer and the employees: A decrease in accidents, turnover, and complaints; an increase in employee morale; and the re-establishment of trust with JR East.

So how did Yabe successfully turn the company around in two years without getting more resources from JR East, hiring better people, or implementing standard work to control process outcomes? According to a *Harvard Business Review* case study, the key to TESSEI's transformation was a focus on implementing a different type of transparency in the organization. By replacing vertical transparency to managers (oversight) with transparency between employees and customers, the company improved the customer experience, motivated and empowered employees to take autonomous action, and most importantly, improved each of the key business metrics.[*]

While Yabe purposely created a transparent and meaningful connection between the customer and the employees, and business results did radically improve within the first two years, Yabe's own words provide us with a much deeper and richer story behind his approach and TESSEI's rise to international fame.[†]

Upon taking over TESSEI, Yabe quickly focused his attention on three areas in need of improvement: profit, finance, and organization. The first area of focus was how to protect the company's profit. JR East was TESSEI's parent company, and it had lost faith in the company and its ability to execute. As a result, JR East began reducing TESSEI's annual budget year over year for a total of $6 million (US). Yabe's first order of business was to determine how to get the money back. His solution: Focus on rebuilding trust through the perfection of the cleaning process itself. As the cleaning work is the main source of revenue, and the Shinkansen cleaning is the highest-profile service offered by TESSEI,[‡] Yabe committed to the transformation of a standardized seven-minute cleaning routine into the "7-Minute Miracle" (as it would be dubbed by CNN later). The second area of focus was the financial. Prior to his arrival, company

---

[*] Ibid., "Trouble at TESSEI," 2.
[†] Teruo Yabe, interview by Michael Martyn, Tokyo, Japan, August 28, 2019.
[‡] TESSEI had a parking lot business and a house cleaning business at that time that were also losing money. Yabe cut the other businesses and focused TESSEI's resources and energy on the Shinkansen cleaning business.

management had become singularly focused on cost reduction in response to the declining revenue. Coupled with sloppy accounting controls in the finance department, Yabe was forced to make a change to top leadership as well as implement new systems and reporting. Finally, Yabe focused on creating and communicating changes to the organizational structure and how management and employees viewed their purpose, role, and priorities at TESSEI. This is where the real work to transform the culture took place. Underlying it all was the need to create a new set of values in the company and use these values to transform TESSEI's relationship with its people, its relationship with the passengers, and finally, its relationship with the parent company.

CHANGING PERCEPTIONS AT TESSEI

The first problem to be addressed was the role of the leader, or how management viewed itself and its function. The previous view of management was directly equated to control. Leading at TESSEI (as in many companies) was all about designing and implementing systems to control individual behaviors, thereby producing the desired result. The seven-minute standard work for cleaning the Shinkansen and the endless company manuals were merely an extension of this philosophy of control. That is, to explicitly define standards for work, train people on how to execute to the standard, and design a management system to ensure that everyone follows the standard each and every time. In this model, there is no opportunity or need for employee input. Subject matter experts had already determined the "best way" to clean the cars within the allotted time of seven minutes as early as 2001. The managers' job was to train the cleaners to the standard and ensure that everyone followed it. The employees' job was simply to follow the instructions perfectly.

Yabe's previous experience as a safety director, however, had taught him a different outlook on the relationship between process control and elimination of variability. According to best practices in behavioral safety, even if the company implemented standard work, rules, and operational procedures for safety, they could not completely eliminate incidents because variability is always present in complex systems and because humans operate machines. At the end of the day, Yabe came to appreciate that part of being human was making mistakes. Therefore, motivating employees to appreciate safety and improving their ability to concentrate is the best way for companies to prevent accidents.

This view of the role of people and the need for motivation was not common prior to Yabe's arrival. In addition to management's view that process control would lead to business results, management viewed employees as a cost rather than an asset and who were capable of adding value over and above following instructions. Rather than valuing people and developing their skills and abilities, management focused their attention on monitoring and correcting employees' attitudes and behaviors. Yabe sought to redefine management and change how TESSEI approached its people, with a focus on individual strengths and expanding their skills and motivation, thus helping each person reach their full potential.

In Yabe's view, every manager in the company needed to see people as capable of great contributions to the organization so long as they are treated with respect and are involved in the structure of their own work. Once managers could admit that people could contribute technical knowledge, interesting ideas, and great wisdom, and would take personal responsibility to achieve their goals, then and only then would it be possible to create a great team that could add value for customers every day. What's more, once people felt that management cared about them and valued their contribution, employees would become excited about their work and naturally change their mindset to be more active in the organization. Once they became more active in the organization, they would feel the benefits of being part of the team and would become more passionate and feel joy. As a result, the company creates a new set of values that will truly embody the spirit of innovation. It is a virtuous cycle that starts with redefining the role of management in the organization.

The second issue Yabe had to confront was how employees viewed themselves and their function. As previously mentioned, the state of employee relations and morale at TESSEI was poor when he arrived. Mistakes and accidents were up year over year, passenger complaints had escalated, and employees felt like second-class citizens in both the eyes of the passengers and the managers. At the heart of the issue was the long-standing belief that if you worked at TESSEI you were nothing more than someone who cleaned up other people's messes on the train. "We are just cleaners" was the overwhelming response from employees when Yabe would ask them about their work and their role in the company. Worse still, the prevailing view was that if you clean trains for your job, it is because you could not get a better job. One employee said, "Customers see me and say to their children, 'Look, if you do not listen to your parents, you will become like them.'"*

If Yabe was to successfully change the role of management as well as spark the passion and participation of the employees, he would have to tackle these perceptions head-on. To do this, he implemented a strategy to redefine the purpose of the work itself while at the same time rebranding the value of team members in the eyes of the passengers. To accomplish this, he started by placing the cause for the current situation squarely at the feet of top management. He told his leaders that it was not the employees' fault that they view themselves as nothing more than cleaners and do not feel a sense of motivation for the work they do each day. Next, he boldly told TESSEI employees:

> I don't want to be rude, but you are working at TESSEI where it is a down-stream in the society. Yet, I don't want you to feel you are inferior. Shinkansen will not run without your cleaning. So, you are not just a cleaning lady or man. JR East Shinkansen is a world-class train with one of the highest technologies. And you are the technical experts to support maintenance by cleaning.†

This reframing of employees from mere cleaners to technical experts who ensure that the world-class Shinkansen runs on time was the first in a series of changes aimed at leveraging the power of words and fostering a sense of pride in one's work at the company. In addition to referring to cleaners as "Technical Experts," the maintenance department was renamed "Technical Services," the cleaning center was renamed the "Service Center," and the Education and Planning Department was renamed the "Hospitality Creation Department." With each change, Yabe instilled a sense of higher purpose in the job and carefully used his words and tone to sound different from the previous leadership group.

TRANSFORMING THE ROLE OF MANAGEMENT

Along with the changes in how employees both physically and attitudinally interacted with the passengers, Yabe launched initiatives aimed at

---

* Bernstein and Buell, "Trouble at TESSEI," 7.
† Teruo Yabe, interview by Michael Martyn, Tokyo, Japan, August 28, 2019.

continuing to transform the role of management at TESSEI. First, he made the solicitation of employee suggestions a part of each manager's job. Second, in order to better engage employees and get results quickly, Yabe focused on the quality of execution rather than the quality of the idea or strategy. "Never say no to constructive proposals from staff," he encouraged. "Even second- and third-rate strategies are fine. Just make sure to have first-rate implementation capabilities."

Next, Yabe set about changing the structure of the environment to more directly link TESSEI employees to the customer and their experience and to continue to break down the perception that employees are just cleaners. The first noticeable change was a change in uniform. As seen in Figure 5.2, Yabe moved away from the old grey uniforms most commonly associated with cleaners and adopted a more modern and stylish uniform.

The change in uniform not only helped instill pride in the employees, but it was an overtly visible sign to passengers that things were changing at TESSEI. This change highlighted another significant improvement in both branding and strategic focus. By 2007, Yabe launched what was affectionately termed "Shinkansen Theatre." From this point on, everything that employees

http://ihcsacafe-en.ihcsa.or.jp/news/tessei/

FIGURE 5.2
TESSEI employees bow to show respect.

did—from the quality of their cleaning to their commitment to creating memories for passengers—would contribute to the well-orchestrated and perfectly executed Shinkansen Theatre. What was truly inspiring about the Shinkansen Theatre was the balance struck between a commitment to best practice standards while simultaneously encouraging each employee to customize the experience for each person who rode the train.

Employees were free to suggest improvements and customize the service and experience they gave to passengers as long as they followed the critical process steps, which allowed each train to be cleaned within the seven-minute window, safely, and with perfect quality. The key to a truly remarkable experience then was to move past the confines of the manual and create *omoide*, or precious memories.

This commitment to Shinkansen Theatre and providing autonomy to employees was a key factor in transforming the standard work for cleaning a Shinkansen train in seven minutes into the "7-Minute Miracle." As Yabe believed, a company that attempts to run exclusively on manuals and push them on people will be a company where people cannot be flexible and make changes that are needed to do great work and adapt to an ever-changing environment. The result is a very rigid and negative organization where people are only allowed to listen to their boss, where new ideas are killed, and where motivation is eventually lost.

Finally, the TESSEI story would be incomplete without a reference to the company's commitment to focusing on strengths and promoting recognition through Angel Reports. This seemingly "nice to have" system provided a simple yet powerful recognition system where managers were expected to lead by example and recognize the contributions employees were making to execute their work with care and create phenomenal customer experiences.

GETTING RESULTS

Within two short years, the transformation was taking hold and the company had seen dramatic improvements in safety, quality, timeliness, and employee morale. More importantly, customers had taken notice and compliments poured in. By 2009, TESSEI experienced a rapid increase in visitors from abroad to witness the 7-Minute Miracle, including the US Secretary of

http://ihcsacafe-en.ihcsa.or.jp/news/tessei/

FIGURE 5.3
TESSEI employees prepare for their shift.

Transportation, the US Ambassador to Japan, and representatives from CNN, NHK, Amtrak, and Southwest Airlines (Figure 5.3).

Perhaps most importantly, employees had more pride in their work, more pride in themselves, and more pride in the company.

> My grandchild [an elementary school student] told me with her eyes shining when I got home. 'Grandma! I saw you on TV! You looked awesome!' You don't know how happy I was. I swallowed my pride and joined this company. But now, we are working actively with new pride.*

TESSEI had successfully transformed what is meant when people say working at the company is a 3K job. Where previously 3K stood for *kitanai*

---

* Ibid.

(dirty), *kitsui* (difficult), and *kiken* (dangerous), it had now come to mean *kansha* (gratitude), *kangeki* (inspiration), and *kendo* (impressiveness).

Since 2009, the company has continued to promote and mature its kaizen culture, improve core processes (they can now do the 7-Minute Miracle in four minutes!), and become a best practice example of *omotenashi* (winning an *omotenashi* award from the Ministry of Economy, Trade and Industry in 2013, a service award from the IT Association in 2014, and the Nihon Service Award from the Minister of Land, Infrastructure, Transport, and Tourism Award in 2018). As a testament to the unique culture TESSEI has created and the impact it is having on the world, the company was benchmarked by more than 350 organizations from 2015 to 2017.

REFLECTIONS ON RESPECT AND HUMILITY AT TESSEI

The story of TESSEI provides us with a great example of not only the power of creating a culture based on respect and humility, but also how the principles of Respect Every Individual and Lead with Humility are valuable in so far as they are embedded as expected behaviors at the systems level. In addition, a careful review of Yabe as a leader reveals a model to which other leaders should aspire. I (Michael Martyn) had the good fortune to spend many hours with Yabe talking about his management philosophy and discussing the real secrets to his success that were not contained in the *Harvard Business Review* case study. When I review my notes from the interviews, the lessons learned look surprisingly like a list of ideal behaviors for the principles of respect and humility.

First, Yabe was explicit with his philosophy of management and the need to put people before profit and passion before performance. This philosophy was steeped in an approach that sought to maximize the engagement of his people (respect) and minimize management's control over the work environment (humility). Second, rather than continue to harp on the standard work of cleaning the train in seven minutes, he rebranded the role of the cleaner and inspired each person to find ways every day to bring joy to their work and create memorable experiences for their customers. Third, due to his background, safety was number one in his mind and a key element of his strategic pillars. Rather than admonish people for mistakes, he challenged them to embrace learning and seek to do better every day. The trust he put in people and the importance he placed on caring for others rapidly turned around the company's poor safety record.

Next, with respect to TESSEI's management systems, his two primary areas of focus were continuous improvement and recognition. Through the use of employee-generated kaizen and the Angel Report program, he put all leaders on notice that the only way the company would be successful was from a top-down and bottom-up transformation. Redefining the role of leadership and creating an inspiring strategy were the top-down elements. But the real power came from empowering and involving everyone in kaizen from the bottom up. Inspiring people with positive words and calling out their great behaviors became a primary role of leadership, and the organizational structure and training programs were redesigned with kaizen and recognition in mind.

Finally, Yabe committed to developing his people at each level of the organization. This development came in the form of skills and leadership training as well as in experiential learning. Both managers and team members alike were encouraged to "try something every day" and experiment with ways to help the company get closer to its vision of providing refreshing, reliable, and heartwarming service through the delivery of Shinkansen Theatre. Everything from his vision, strategy, philosophy, and execution embodies the behaviors of Respect Every Individual and Lead with Humility.

PRIDE IN ONE'S WORK

Teruo Yabe, former chairman of TESSEI, said, "People can find new hopes and dreams by reconfirming and accepting their true roles and missions." The true strength of TESSEI lies in its Cleaning Angels. The diligence of the Angels is not limited to their daily work. The goal is to provide "total service to passengers," covering almost everything other than technical areas and train operation. The Angels pursue their work with the determination to do everything possible to keep passengers feeling content and at home. According to Yabe, they also come up with a steady stream of insights, ideas, and ingenuity in striving to improve operations and enhance the quality of service.

6

Systems That Support Cultural Enablers

We can't impose our will on a system. We can listen to what the system tells us and discover how its properties and our values can work together to bring forth something much better than could have ever been produced by our will alone.

—Donella Meadows*

We have talked at length about the principles of respect and humility, the four supporting concepts, and the behaviors we strive to embed in the actions of our leaders, managers, and associates. Now we turn our attention to the critical systems that enable us to embed these behaviors into each area of our organization and each element of our work.

As referenced in Chapter 1, the *Shingo Model* clearly illustrates the role systems play in developing a world-class culture. If we recognize the Shingo Institute's three insights of organizational excellence that (1) results require ideal behaviors, (2) purpose and systems drive behavior, and (3) principles inform ideal behavior, then no book on enabling your culture would be complete without a review of the key systems required. It is important to note, however, that our review of key systems is by no means exhaustive. As any system can be built in a way that emphasizes respect and humility in its design and execution, enabling culture through systems is a holistic exercise. That being said, there are five key systems that will be discussed here. Each of these systems is critical from the standpoint of encouraging the ideal behaviors aligned with the principles found in the Cultural Enablers dimension. In addition, each of these

---

* Donella H. Meadows, *Thinking in Systems: A Primer* (Chelsea Green Publishing, 2008).

DOI: 10.4324/9781003425519-6

systems is considered foundational from the perspective of assessing an organization's cultural maturity.

To understand why certain systems are more important than others for enabling culture, let's first summarize some of the key lessons that come out of our review of the principles of Respect Every Individual and Lead with Humility. In organizations where both principles are deeply embedded, we see cultures where people feel respected, trusted, and appreciated. We see leaders who are open to the ideas of others, who are transparent about their strengths and weaknesses, and who are committed to developing a learning environment. When respected and led with humility, people have the opportunity to flourish and reach their potential through the mastery of their work and contribution to continuous improvement. Armed with the knowledge of what respect and humility look like in an organization, it is a leader's role to ensure that the systems we choose to implement, and the design of the systems, reflect the focus on these drivers of culture.

WHAT PEOPLE WANT FROM CULTURE

To maximize the impact of these two principles through the design and implementation of key systems, we must remember what people want from an engaged and empowered culture.

- **Connect to a larger purpose:** People want to be aligned with the purpose of the organization. As seen in the Gallup research, believing in the organizational mission, vision, and values is becoming more important to employees. Because of this, it is critical that you overtly communicate what your purpose is in addition to clearly articulating the purpose of each system you employ and the ideal behaviors you define. An organization's strategy, communications, recruiting, onboarding, and ongoing training can all have an effect on how an organization defines and aligns its purpose.
- **Part of a community:** In addition to aligning their personal purpose with the organization's purpose, people also strive to become a member of a meaningful community. This community includes not only the immediate team members and leaders an individual comes into contact with during a typical workday, but also the community

in which the organization operates. Whether that community represents customers, suppliers, or the broader community, what is important is that everyone has the opportunity to feel a part of that community and that membership in the community is meaningful. An organization's onboarding, coaching, recognition, and opportunities for service all work to help create, reinforce, and deepen the sense of community.

- **Feel physically and psychologically safe:** As mentioned in the discussion on supporting concepts, the need to create a safe environment is the first priority. Safe environments include ensuring physical safety as well as psychological safety. Organizations that focus on developing a safe culture build high levels of trust and loyalty in their people. Keeping everyone safe is not only the right thing to do, but it also serves to improve engagement and build a culture of respect. An organization's safety systems, environmental efforts, commitment to employee well-being, and coaching system are all examples of ways that health and safety are made a priority and continuously improved.

- **Regular and honest feedback:** People want and need open and honest feedback. In fact, research has shown that people want feedback even if it is not always positive. The most important criteria are that it is honest and timely. One of the primary drivers of job dissatisfaction is not knowing where you stand with an organization and if your job performance and contribution are valued and appreciated. The effectiveness with which an organization and its leaders utilize a multi-faceted approach to providing feedback has a direct correlation to employee satisfaction and engagement. An organization's coaching system, visual management, communication strategy, leader standard work, and recognition system are all part of this integrated approach.

- **Opportunities for growth and development:** Coupled with regular and honest feedback, people want growth and development opportunities. These opportunities can be work- and career-related, or opportunities for personal growth outside of work. The type of opportunity is not as critical as having the opportunity for growth itself. The key is creating an environment where each individual can challenge him or herself to grow as a person and as a professional. In our experience, the best opportunities for development are driven by the individuals themselves and are supported through participative leadership and a resource commitment from the organization. As it was to providing feedback, the coaching system is critical for creating an environment committed to development. In addition to coaching, an organization's training and development systems, its use of mentors, and its on-the-job skills training all contribute to an environment that provides people with opportunities to grow and better themselves as a regular part of their work.

- **Opportunities to make positive contributions:** Finally, each individual must be trusted and empowered to make positive contributions to the organization's success. These contributions can come in the form of doing a great job in their daily work (acknowledged through the recognition system) or in the form of participating in the organization's efforts to help support the community and take care of the environment. The variety and options for people to contribute really are endless. That being said, one of the often-overlooked areas of contribution, and the primary driver of engagement an individual feels, is participating in continuous improvement activities. The ability to identify and solve problems and help the organization accomplish its goals is a great source of pride for people and helps enable the right type of culture. As such, an organization's problem-solving system is critical, along with standard follow-up, from leaders that support the removal of roadblocks and aligning people's passions with opportunities for improving performance.

THE FIVE KEY SYSTEMS

Now let's turn our attention to the key systems that organizations must implement in order to enable a world-class culture. Remember, while there is no "one best way" to design a system and select the tools that will enable the system, each of the following systems must work together to accomplish both business goals and cultural goals. In addition, there are any number of systems that organizations will employ to get results and contribute to their culture. We applaud any effort to employ systems that reinforce respect and humility and that contribute to the long-term success of the organization. The Shingo Institute provides more guidance on systems thinking in the Systems Design workshop and the *Systems Design** book. These resources highlight system types and system components, including the required communication tools. For our purposes, we have only included those systems that, from a Shingo examiner's perspective, would be viewed as required.†

SYSTEM #1: ENVIRONMENTAL, HEALTH, AND SAFETY

The first of our five systems is composed of three distinct, yet complementary elements: Environmental work, health and wellness, and safety. Let's start first by looking at what characterizes a good safety system that aids in enabling a culture of respect. At a minimum, organizations need a specific system that addresses safety incidents and potential future issues at the behavioral level. A good safety system not only sets goals for improvement, but also tracks its effectiveness at both the results level and the behavioral level. This means that the system is held accountable for its results, such as the number of incidents, worker's compensation claims, and lost time days. It also tracks the key behavioral indicators that enable an organization to ensure it is proactive in its efforts to avoid safety issues before they occur.

Example: Forest Tosara Baldoyle, Ireland

Established in 1984, Forest Tosara Ltd., Baldoyle is a 33,000-square-foot manufacturing plant, producing over 3.3 million kilograms of Sudocrem per year and shipping the product worldwide. Sudocrem is a water-in-oil emulsion cream used in the treatment of various skin conditions including diaper rash, eczema, acne, and pressure sores. The Baldoyle site won the Shingo Bronze Medallion in 2018.

---

* Brent R. Allen and April A. Bosworth, eds., *Systems Design: Building Systems that Drive Ideal Behavior* (New York, NY: Routledge, 2021).

† It is important to note that with the exception of perhaps Environmental, Health, and Safety, the five key systems have not been presented here in order of importance or impact. From a cultural standpoint, consider the systems on this as equally important and necessary in your journey to world class. In addition, we have chosen to label the systems in a manner consistent with how Shingo Examiners typically assess and provide feedback to an organization. For example, an organization could choose to define EH&S as three distinct "systems."

Assuring a safe working environment for its employees has always been the company's number one responsibility and priority. It is critical to Forest Tosara Baldoyle that each leader and manager respect all of its team members so that they leave work in the same condition as they arrived. While the company traditionally relied on procedures and engineering solutions to eliminate hazards, the focus shifted to using these existing tools along with modifying the behavior of employees to eliminate unsafe practices. It was only through developing a culture of safe practices and employee behavior that the company could ensure a sustained safe working environment for all.

Orla O'Callahan, Environment, Health and Safety (EH&S) specialist at Forest Tosara, said, "Ideal behavior means challenging all aspects of my work and helping our employees succeed in doing things in a safe manner by sustaining the right behavior through positive reinforcement."

To this end, Forest Tosara developed the Target Zero program, where all team members are encouraged to focus on behavior. The program highlights the hidden impact of incidents, awareness, and how behaviors can reduce unnecessary accidents, ensuring a secure and safer environment at work and at home.

As an example of this new program, which began in January 2016, all the daily and weekly meetings began with a safety moment (Figure 6.1) as the first item on the agenda. A safety moment is a brief discussion on a safety-related topic that is communicated weekly, ensuring that team members are aware of their own safety at work and their family's safety at home. Each week a different safety moment theme is generated and discussed across the site and is the first item on the agenda at all meetings, huddles, and teleconferences. In addition to informing employees about specific safety issues, they also contribute to a corporate safety culture and behaviors that reinforce safe practices.

Example: Abbott in Ireland and the Croí an Óir Program

Home to nearly 3,000 employees across nine sites, Abbott in Ireland is dedicated to communities, both large and small, and seeks to make a significant and long-lasting difference in the quality of people's lives. From helping the school children of Longford explore the wonders of science to modernizing the healthcare infrastructure in Tanzania, Abbott employees have been supporting schools and local community groups in Longford in innovative ways for more than a decade.

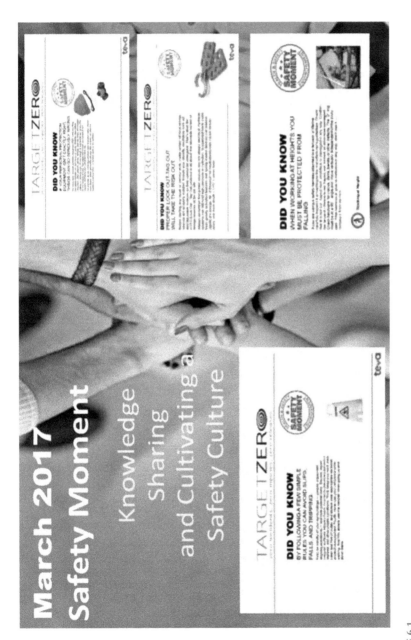

FIGURE 6.1
Example of a Safety Moment poster used at Forest Tosara.

The year 2017 marked the tenth year of Abbott's Croí an Óir program and its impact has been significant. The Croí an Óir program, which means "Heart of Gold," was created to support the commitment of Abbott employees across the country to give back to their local communities. Each Abbott site ensures that a range of organizations are supported throughout the year with a local and national focus. Activities range from career talks, science experiments, gardening, fun runs, fundraising for local charities, and much more. Nationwide, Croí has delivered more than 70,000 volunteer hours, and the program has had a tremendous impact.

Nowhere has the spirit of Croí been more evident than in Longford, where some of the highlights have included:

- Abbott Family Science, which engages primary school students, their parents, and teachers in learning about science through fun experiments. More than 600 Abbott volunteers have been involved in engaging more than 5,000 students and families in education programs in Ireland since 2009. Every year, Abbott in Longford hosts Family Science events where families are encouraged to explore science concepts beyond the classroom.
- Junior Achievement: Abbott employees have used their skills and expertise to deliver innovative enterprise and life skills programs in more than 100 schools since the partnership began in 2003. Abbott seeks to make a significant and long-lasting difference to people's lives in the communities in which it operates. To that end, it has developed and fostered this long-term partnership with Junior Achievement Ireland.
- Employees have been supporting the Abbott Fund program to modernize Tanzania's healthcare infrastructure. Over recent years, experts have volunteered their time, knowledge, and skills to help train and mentor local laboratory teams. Their primary objectives are to implement an integrated IT system for patient registration and lab sample management, and to train local staff to use the system.

Ciaran Corcoran, site director at Abbott Longford, said,

At Abbott, we believe that being engaged and active in the community is beneficial to living a healthy and happy life. That is why we support volunteering and have put corporate citizenship at the heart of our business.

We are proud of everything our teams have achieved across Ireland and especially in Longford over the past ten years. This milestone is a tremendous motivation to do more in the future, and the teams are continuing to put a big focus on working with young people to encourage their interest in science, technology, math, and engineering. By sparking an interest in science with young people early in their lives, Abbott aims to provide a foundation for the next generation of scientific leaders to shape the future of innovation.

Example: Hologic Costa Rica

Hologic is an innovative medical technology company focused on advancing women's health and well-being through early detection and treatment of health problems, such as breast cancer and reproductive disorders. This approach is known as "The Science of Sure." At Hologic Costa Rica, the site manufactures disposable medical devices.

Recipient of the Shingo Prize in 2022, Hologic Costa Rica is committed to creating an environment of respect by developing a physically and emotionally safe workplace and by taking care of the environment. Following are examples of the work the organization has done to be environmentally responsible and to reduce the negative impact of its operations.

In 2018, the ideal behavior of taking care of the environment was supported by eliminating all of the waste baskets and replacing them with recycling stations located in strategic places in the office areas. After incorporating employee recommendations (in alignment with the principle "I Listen and Learn"), there are now a total of nine different types of waste cans: Paper, organic, plastic, aluminum, landfill waste, tetra pack, COVID-19, batteries, and isopropyl alcohol (IPA) wipes. That improvement transformed the way employees understood waste treatment and was the trigger to redefining recycling waste routes, thus promoting a continuously increasing rate of recycling from 66 percent to 83 percent in 2021.

In 2018, the site began a campaign to reuse packaging material, which was made available for employees to take home. To date, more than 254 tons of packaging material have been reused by Hologic's employees as part of this circular economy proposal.

Further in FY19, the photovoltaic system was installed. This project reduces energy consumption by the equivalent of 344 Costa Rican households, which is equal to an annual reduction of $70,000 and 280 tons in carbon footprint. In FY20, the implementation of the energy management system was completed according to ISO 50001.

Finally, Hologic Costa Rica's efforts to be good stewards of the environment have led to external awards. The site is the recipient of the Bandera Azul (Blue Flag), an award given every year to recognize efforts related to environmental protection. In addition, Hologic Costa Rica has received a climate change prevention award two years in a row (for 2019 and 2020).

SYSTEM #2: TRAINING AND DEVELOPMENT

The training and development system is meant to directly address the skills and capabilities organizations need to have in place to provide timely and quality products and services to their customers. In addition, a good training and development system encourages personal growth and development opportunities, in conjunction with the coaching system. It also provides training and development aimed at improving the problem-solving skills of each employee. To accomplish this, there should be formal training and educational opportunities for employees to learn about the principles, systems, and tools of continuous improvement. While the format, content, and medium of this training can vary, care should be taken to ensure that adult learning principles are honored and that a significant portion of the time is devoted to applying the lessons learned in the work environment.

Leaders and managers also provide opportunities for team member development in a number of ways. First, they involve each team member in improving the work and ensuring that all employees explore new ideas without the fear of failure. Second, leaders and managers treat all ideas as equal in value no matter whose idea it is, and they encourage (and track) participation from everyone in the organization. Leaders further encourage growth for employees by creating opportunities for them to gain insight by engaging people from outside their own areas in order to share ideas, discuss issues, and observe best practices. Finally, leaders and managers create an environment of open and honest two-way communication throughout the organization, which fosters trust and connection, thereby allowing team members to embrace their own personal opportunities to grow and help the organization succeed.

Example: Viatris Damastown, Ireland

Viatris is a global pharmaceutical company that employs 35,000 people and is committed to providing access to high-quality medicine in more than 165 countries and territories. The Damastown site in Dublin manufactures active ingredients and solid oral-dosage finished products for worldwide distribution. The site has achieved substantial industry recognition for its operational excellence journey and was a recipient of the Shingo Silver Medallion in 2016.

Viatris Damastown is committed to developing their people with a "Grow Our Own" approach. Following are examples of the work the organization has done to develop people through education and training programs.

Because Viatris Damastown leadership recognizes that first impressions can be crucial to a new hire's ongoing success with the company, employees participate in a robust two-day induction process. The training covers health and safety, manual handling, good manufacturing practices (GMP), an introduction to values and behaviors and the *Shingo Model*, the organizational structure, and a tour of the facility. Following the induction period, all new team members are assigned a mentor from within their departments to be their points of contact. The mentors are available for advice and support over the first few weeks of transitioning into the workplace.

The organization further recognizes the importance of investing in people to realize the Viatris Damastown business strategy. To that end, Viatris provides ongoing opportunities for education, personal development, and training. Each year, they look at organizational requirements and available resources to make sure the necessary skillsets are available to achieve the objectives. This review gives rise to the annual training plan, which is a dynamic document where each section is prepared by the relevant department manager and compiled into a single plan by HR. The overall plan considers business needs, individual aspirations, and professional requirements. It also identifies all proposed training, including safety, management "soft" skills, and Lean manufacturing training, such as Six Sigma, A3 problem-solving, and total productive maintenance. The annual training plan serves as a working document and guides throughout the year and is subject to change as new requirements materialize.

The Further Education Policy complements the annual training plan by promoting attendance at relevant external courses. Between 2010 and 2015, 48 employees received further educational funding. Given that Viatris Damastown has a "Grow Our Own" approach in relation to talent management, the site actively encourages all employees to further their education by providing a 100-percent level of funding for all relevant courses. Also, paid time off is provided to complete external examinations.

Aligned with the Shingo supporting concept, Develop People, some departments have incorporated learning and development activities into their overall structure. In operations, for example, in order for production team members to progress from one level to the next, they must complete all of the learning tasks associated with their existing level. Each level has additional learning and development tasks that improve the team members' versatility and ultimately their ability to move into a process or line lead position and possibly into another department, such as technical or quality assurance. Similar structures for employee progression exist within maintenance and quality control. Viatris Damastown now has a number of employees on site who have, through the deployment of the organization's learning and development process, progressed through different departments and functions and now hold a supervisory or management position. Naturally, the business benefits from the promotion of colleagues as they bring a cross-functional knowledge that can only help from a developmental perspective, both personal and professional. In addition, internally promoted people are motivated to drive future improvements in their areas of expertise.

The "Grow Our Own" approach also provides the organization with a very clear line of sight for effective succession planning. Wherever possible, the company releases people from their day-to-day jobs into project roles. Involving their own people in projects has proved highly beneficial in building capability, developing future leaders, and reducing reliance on external contractors. Although it is not possible to provide everyone with a linear career development plan, the site is engaged in providing developmental opportunities for employees by participation in projects and cross-functional teams when such opportunities arise.

Finally, Viatris Damastown has ensured that every employee is able to record learning and development time as Continuous Professional

Development (CPD) hours. This ability is directly linked to obtaining CPD recognition from Engineers Ireland, the professional body for Ireland. Initially introduced in the technical department, Viatris has extended the standard to the entire site, which ensures that all learning and development activities focus on the courses that attain CPD hours. This is a huge benefit to the people and to the organization as it enables everyone to manage their own development and provides a ready measure of dedicated training hours on specific subjects.

SYSTEM #3: CONTINUOUS IMPROVEMENT

A robust continuous improvement system plays a prominent role in the Continuous Improvement dimension of the *Shingo Model* and in the organization as it works to improve all of the other systems within it. While continuous improvement in this context focuses more on the method of problem-solving, the use of facts and data, and the presence of scientific thinking in the approach, continuous improvement activities are also a primary driver of an engaged culture. In addition, participation in continuous improvement is a critical measure of cultural maturity, both qualitatively and quantitatively. In a mature culture of organizational excellence, continuous improvement is evident through high levels of engagement, as witnessed by employees at all levels of the organization identifying, owning, and solving problems every day.

With respect to the system itself, it is critical that the execution of ownership and operation of the process from end to end be managed at the team level whenever possible. Empowering teams to own the process demonstrates respect for every individual. In addition, to maximize engagement, all employees need to be trusted to make decisions and take responsibility for their improvement activities. Trusting their ideas and allowing them to make decisions that ultimately affect the course of the organization demonstrates leading with humility.

It is also important that the continuous improvement system be structured and follow a defined approach that leverages scientific thinking and makes it easy to solve simple and complex problems. That being said, the power of continuous improvement to engage a culture lies in the amount of ownership an individual is trusted to take and the speed at which ideas turn into actions and actions turn into improvements in performance. The more leadership does to co-create a system that allows every person in the organization to see something, say something, and do something about it every day, the higher the participation and the higher the level of engagement.

Example: University of Washington, Seattle, Washington

Beginning in 2010, the University of Washington Finance and Facilities departments sought to implement a Lean cultural transformation as a comprehensive way to address changing customer demands and reduced operation budgets. Finance and Facilities were comprised of a diverse group of operational and financial units of the university and accounted for 1,400 of the university's employees. To do this, leadership embraced a larger purpose: "To develop our people, to design our culture, to deliver our results."[*]

As part of the pursuit of their vision, the university made a substantial commitment to developing their people and trusting them to identify and solve problems every day. During a period of eight years, 242 areas were launched on a journey of continuous improvement, over 8,000 hours of training and development were provided to employees, and 47 internal coaches were developed to assist team members in their continuous improvement activities.

One of the key systems they implemented was the daily kaizen system. The daily kaizen system operated within the structure of the management system and focused on the process of generating, prioritizing, implementing, and celebrating continuous improvement ideas. The design of the system was kept simple to allow for ease of scaling and speed of implementation. Co-creation was the key to designing the system to model the principles of Respect Every Individual and Lead with Humility. Through co-creative design, the university shared the responsibility for the design, implementation, and sustainment of the system with the teams, thereby maximizing participation. When doing this, they found a 70/30 split to be a generally good balance. Seventy percent of the elements

---

[*] Michael Martyn, Mark McKenzie, and Doug Merrill, "Transforming Higher Ed: Implementing a Culture of Continuous Improvement at the University of Washington, 2010–2018." (Portland, OR: SISU Consulting Group, 2019). This case study received the Shingo Research Award in 2019.

and behaviors needed to be successful with a daily kaizen system are principle-based and have been proven to work overtime. Thirty percent of the elements and behaviors must actively be tailored to the environment to work properly or redesigned altogether. This approach resulted in more than 80,000 implemented employee ideas and $328 million in financial benefit to the University.

SYSTEM #4: COACHING

A good coaching system encompasses two primary activities. First, leaders and managers should have standard work that encourages spending time in the gemba with their people, understanding reality, and having the opportunity to both formally and informally coach on a case-by-case basis. Ideally, the opportunities to be out with your people should be structured around a daily routine, allowing you to frequently be in the workplace observing actual processes, understanding problems and opportunities, and continually providing coaching for problem-solving. Leaders and managers spending time in the gemba make sure that the problems and solutions that a team is identifying are considered from a broad (systems) perspective, and those leaders focus on asking supportive questions rather than giving answers or solutions. In addition, the more time leaders spend in the gemba supporting the success of their people through planned and unplanned interactions, the greater the trust they build and the deeper connection with their people and their problems. The goal is to achieve a partnership between leadership and team members where clear goals and objectives, combined with a daily management system that is focused on solving problems, create an environment where leaders are viewed as coaches that help to remove roadblocks and create the ability for teams to "own their business."

The second activity that is critical to building an engaging coaching system is one-on-one coaching. One-on-one coaching is an opportunity for leaders to get to know their team members on a personal and professional level and to build trust through a regularly scheduled and structured process. The coaching is conducted at a pre-determined frequency, most commonly once per month, although many of our clients have matured to doing coaching on a weekly basis. The exact frequency is not as important as keeping the schedule, coming prepared for each session, and closing the loop on follow-up actions. Good coaching finds a balance between allowing the coaches to self-direct the activities and the leader holding the team member accountable for keeping their commitments to themselves and accomplishing their goals.

Example: US Synthetic, Orem, Utah

Founded in 1978, US Synthetic, a ChampionX company, is the leading provider of polycrystalline diamond cutters (PDCs) for oil and gas exploration. The company has more than 700 employees in the Orem, Utah, site and more than $200 million in annual sales. US Synthetic received the Shingo Prize in 2011.

Over the years, the company has developed a powerful coaching system that focuses on the individual and aligns with the company's vision to "Improve Lives." After an employee has been onboarded, trained, and assimilated into an area, he or she starts regular one-on-one sessions with the team lead to discuss progress and goals relating to the employee's personal strategy. There is also time for unstructured discussion and support for any issues the employee may be experiencing.

Sessions are held monthly and typically last 30 minutes. Leaders are free to conduct the sessions wherever is most comfortable to the employee and coaching sessions can often be seen in the cafeteria or on the basketball court. The coaching discussions include recognition and value, effective management, engagement in process improvement work, performance, communication, a review of action items, and a discussion of development and goals. Every employee is encouraged to have a vision for their future in the company and to generate action items connected to realizing that future. Leaders are given training and development in knowing how to connect with their team members and conduct effective coaching sessions.

The entire coaching process and results are documented and kept in a file, which contains coaching records, training certifications, and any projects or kaizen the employee is working on. The folder also contains development plans and goals the employee is striving to reach. The development plans and goals can be career related or of a personal nature. In fact, some of the most powerful stories about the power of this coaching system come from personal transformations such as eliminating an addiction, graduating from college, or saving a marriage.

SYSTEM #5: RECOGNITION

Recognition is an important part of creating an environment that demonstrates respect. Giving credit to others is also a characteristic of humble leaders. Unfortunately, good recognition is not easy to find, and it is a skill that needs to be developed by most leaders. The act of providing timely, personalized, and meaningful recognition requires leaders who spend time getting to know their people, believe in the power of appreciation, and utilize a range of methods to ensure that recognition activities stay fresh and motivating in the minds of their people.

In our experience, good recognition systems have some common characteristics. First, there are defined criteria for receiving recognition. This doesn't mean that unstructured or spontaneous recognition is not encouraged or active. What it does mean is that organizational leadership has partnered with their people to determine the type of behaviors that are valued most and has integrated these behaviors into a formal recognition process. Next, while individuals may prefer how they want to be recognized—and that should be honored—in general, public displays of recognition are the most powerful. Every organization we have worked with that has a world-class recognition system finds ways to overtly visualize the system and put a name and face to the recognition. Making the recognition visual and public shows everyone in the organization what good behavior looks like and can create healthy social pressure among peers to get recognized.

Next, it is critical that the recognition be timely. Years ago, Ken Blanchard counseled readers of *The One Minute Manager* to "catch them doing something right,"* then publicly praise them. This is still sound advice.

The recognition should be specific and individualized, stating what the person did, why it was important, and if possible, what it did to help the team, group, or organization. With respect to who should be doing the recognition, strive to create a balance between manager recognition and peer-to-peer recognition. While it is important for leaders to recognize their people, research has shown that peer recognition creates more satisfaction than recognition coming from a manager. People feel more

---

* Kenneth Blanchard, *The One Minute Manager* (New York, NY: Berkley Publishing, 1981), 35.

pride in knowing that their peers value what they do and took the time to recognize them.

One last word of caution. While providing gifts, company merchandise, or even money can be part of an effective recognition, be careful how heavily you tie your program to extrinsic rewards. True engagement comes from the intrinsic motivation of being valued for a contribution, taking pride in the work, and being inspired to help build a culture in which everyone can be proud.

Karen Ackerman, VP of Human Resources at Centra Health, described the change she has seen in her organization's culture through intrinsic motivation. She said,

> There is now the expectation that we appreciate great work. Appreciation has become a part of who we are. People use that word and talk about it. It's part of the heartbeat of our organization, and it provides all of us hope when we see the good things people are doing across the organization.

Example: OC Tanner, Salt Lake City, Utah

Founded in 1927, OC Tanner has more than 1,600 employees and annual revenues of more than $600 million. The company's mission is to help companies appreciate people who do great work—because celebrating great work inspires people to invent, to create, and to discover. And when people are inspired, companies grow. The company has great employee retention, with the average tenure for team members at 7.5 years.

At OC Tanner, recognition and appreciation of their own employees are part of who they are at their core. The Appreciate Great People program was designed to encourage every employee at OC Tanner to recognize their fellow employees. Leaders proclaim that "those closest to the work know what's best." If any employee sees outstanding performance, they can instantly nominate that individual or team for recognition. Even the newest employees can nominate anyone for the highest awards.*

OC Tanner's service award program and its performance program are called Appreciate Great in Culture Cloud.† It is an entirely web-

---

* Sami Ahmed, "OC Tanner: Shingo Model of Continued Success" (Huntsman Teaching Case Series, Utah State University, Logan, UT, September 2018).

† OC Tanner, "Appreciate Great in Culture Cloud" (New Hire PowerPoint presentation, OC Tanner, Salt Lake City, UT).

based program, and each employee receives a personal budget, which is updated every quarter, to use to reward others for great work. The budget is 300 points and is used for non-monetary recognition. In addition to the budget, each employee receives an orientation and training on the recognition program and guidance on best practices.

Best Practices for the "Appreciate Great in Culture Cloud" Program

Give It Meaning: Recognize work that delivers impact and aligns with company goals.

Celebrate Progress: Celebrate the little victories not just the big wins.

Appreciate Results: Pay attention to work that innovates and enhances the company's business practices.

Frequent: Recognize often. According to Gallup, every seven days is best.

Timely: Don't wait. Give it as soon after the accomplishment as possible.

Inclusive: Celebrate team members based on their own strengths. You shouldn't focus only on the superstars.

Performance-Based: Give recognition for a specific achievement or contribution and tie it to the company values.

Using these best practices as a guide, employees can award eCards without points for day-to-day effort as well as to offer encouragement, welcome new team members, and celebrate birthdays or other life events.

Employees can also nominate anyone for an award (Bronze, Silver, Gold, or Platinum). These nominations need to be approved, but they come with a certificate and points that can be redeemed for merchandise. Finally, OC Tanner celebrates career achievement with symbolic awards and yearbooks based on years of service.

DESIGN FOR ELEGANCE AND ENGAGEMENT

Industrial designer, author, and activist Victor J. Papanick wrote, "The only important thing about design is how it relates to people."* Systems can quickly become overly complicated and work contrary

---

* Victor J. Papanick, *Design for the Real World: Human Ecology and Social Change* (New York, NY: Pantheon Books, 1972).

to your goal of enabling an engaged culture. When designing systems, your goal is to achieve elegance in design, be iterative in your development, and involve your people in creating and improving the system itself over time. In addition, regardless of the system you are designing, there are four common characteristics that must be present for the design to be effective (results and behaviors) and sustainable. First, you must clearly establish the purpose of the system. Second, you must define measurable outcomes with which to accurately assess the results of the system. Third, each system must have clearly defined standards for execution. Finally, the system must be visual and easy to adhere to and evaluate.

7

Assessing the Cultural Enablers Dimension

The Shingo Institute has been conducting site visits and administering the Shingo Prize for almost four decades. In that time, they have learned many lessons about how to conduct a good assessment as well as what a world-class organization looks like. The assessment process itself consists of numerous distinct stages and can involve hundreds, if not thousands, of hours of work to prepare the site, write an achievement report, and host a site visit. Aside from the work that goes into the Shingo challenge itself, there is tremendous effort invested by the organization in terms of systems optimization, communication, continuous improvement, and training and development.

With each of these activities, understanding what you want from your culture and what it looks like when you get there is critical. That is where implementing an effective assessment process is key. If you understand where you are relative to where you want to be, you have established the gap and can determine what you need to do to close the gap to achieve organizational excellence.

But what if you are not interested in challenging for the Shingo Prize? If you are interested solely in developing a great culture but have no intention of challenging for the Shingo Prize, you are in good company. Actually, the vast majority of organizations who use the *Shingo Model* never challenge for the prize. Regardless, if you see a Shingo Prize challenge in your organization's future, understanding the *Shingo Model* and, more importantly, understanding how to assess your own cultural maturity is critical to identifying and closing gaps in performance. And while our purpose in this book is not to teach

DOI: 10.4324/9781003425519-7

you how to become an experienced examiner or to conduct a formal Shingo assessment, understanding the fundamentals of behavioral assessments is immensely valuable.

So how do you assess whether or not your culture is exhibiting behaviors of respect and humility on a daily basis? And how does your maturity stack up relative to the ideal? These are the fundamental questions that should form the basis of your assessment process. They also represent the intersection between your vision for your culture and the *Shingo Model's* approach to evaluating maturity. Once you can understand what it means to exhibit respect and humility ideally and can see how you compare to this ideal, you have the ability to create an implementation roadmap for improvement.

When attempting to answer these questions, there are numerous ways you could approach assessing the presence and maturity of the behaviors of respect and humility seen in your culture. First, you could choose to have a mock Shingo assessment. We have conducted hundreds of these over the years for our clients. When we do this assessment, we put on our Shingo examiner hats and conduct it in the same manner, tone, and presentation as we would if the organization were actually challenging for the Shingo Prize. The process is intense, the experience mirrors an actual Shingo site visit, and the feedback report provides an in-depth analysis of each dimension of the *Shingo Model*. Best practices from our clients are included in the recommendations and an implementation roadmap is customized and co-created for each client.

If that type of assessment is more of a commitment than you are ready for, there are other ways to begin to see where your culture is and how to improve it. Many of our clients use cultural surveys as a means to begin to see the gap. Some clients elect to administer Shingo Insight.* Shingo Insight is a web-delivered assessment that looks at the entire organization— executives, managers, and team members—and compares their behaviors against the *Shingo Model*. The assessment covers all three dimensions of the *Shingo Model* and is quite extensive. While some organizations start here, the majority of our clients use Shingo Insight when they get closer to the level of maturity where they plan to challenge for the Shingo Prize.

Regardless of the method you choose to assess your organization, your systems, and your principle-based behaviors, we recommend

---

* For more information on Shingo Insight, visit shingo.org/insight.

you focus your next steps in three areas: (1) define the ideal behaviors you will focus on, (2) design an effective assessment process, and (3) evaluate your organization's behavioral maturity using Shingo's FISDR methodology.

IDENTIFY YOUR IDEAL BEHAVIORS

In this book, we have discussed the principles required to enable your culture, the supporting concepts underlying those principles, and the behavioral benchmarks established by the Shingo Institute based on more than 35 years of research, assessment, and observation in some of the world's best organizations. We have also given you some ideal behaviors that many of our past Shingo Prize–recipient clients exhibit on a daily basis.

That being said, it is important to note that there is no master set of ideal behaviors. The *Shingo Model* and its principles don't work that way. In fact, the best companies we have worked with study the principles and supporting concepts deeply, benchmark other world-class organizations, and then commit the time and energy to identify the ideal behaviors that the principles have informed through their own study. When done well, these ideal behaviors align with and strengthen their values, and embody the behavioral benchmarks found within the *Shingo Model*. We strongly recommend that you consider doing the same and that you involve a representative cross section of your employees in the process of agreeing on the ideal behaviors to focus on. In doing so, you will ensure that the wider organization will feel a stronger sense of ownership of the agreed behaviors.

The first step in assessing the maturity of your own culture is defining with clarity what behaviors you want to see (ideal) and what those behaviors will look like when they move toward the ideal. Moving *toward* the ideal implies that behavior will mature along a continuum. The organization will not move from the current state to the ideal in one step. Identifying Key Behavioral Indicators (KBIs) to measure progress along the continuum will help with an assessment. The following is an example of the process that one of our Shingo Award–recipient clients used to create and deploy their own set of ideal behaviors.

Example: Boston Scientific, Cork, Ireland

In 1997, Boston Scientific acquired a 30-acre site in Cork, Ireland, that included a 25,000 square-foot facility featuring a historic protected building, the Munster Institute. Currently, the company operates a 195,000 square-foot production facility, of which 74,000 square feet is a controlled environment. The site serves four divisions of the overall Boston Scientific business: Peripheral Intervention, Endoscopy, Interventional Cardiology, and Urology and Pelvic Health. In order to serve its customers, the site runs a two-shift operation with approximately 800 employees, and it manufactures 5.4 million units per year across 37 product lines. Boston Scientific Cork received the Shingo Prize in 2016.

Boston Scientific Cork has a rich history in improvement systems that date back to 2001. Starting in 2010, however, the site shifted its focus from the implementation of Lean tools to the development of a culture of continuous improvement. Establishing ideal behaviors was a huge milestone in their journey. The process of establishing ideal behaviors started with a small team in the carbapenem-resistant Enterobacterales (CRE) clean room, but there was a general consensus that ideal behaviors needed to become a way of life at the site after the pilot group drafted a set of behaviors and held each other accountable through peer-to-peer feedback and support.

It was then agreed that the whole indirect population should meet in a forum and discuss what they felt the ideal behaviors should be. This group developed the site's ideal behavior vision: "I want to be here. I do my best work here." This vision became the backbone of Cork's ideal behaviors. In April 2014, more than 170 indirect employees took part in a series of Café Conversations on ideal behaviors. The objective was to communicate current ideal behaviors, collaborate, and gain consensus on the right set of behaviors to live by. There were eight sessions, each involving two facilitators and four table hosts who chaired discussions on the following four questions:

1. To be the kind of place you look forward to getting up and coming into every morning, what would the behaviors in this workplace need to be?
2. How would you maintain the ideal behaviors and hold others to the same standards during challenging times?

3. What does trust at work mean to you?
4. What one thing would you do or stop doing that would help you live the ideal behaviors and create a positive impact on others?

The Café Conversations fostered dialogue and created a dynamic network of conversation to shape the site's future together. They motivated people to act like owners of change by working together to create a shared initiative to influence their work environment. There was strong engagement from cross-functional team members. Forty-two people were facilitators or hosts and they championed ideal behaviors with a strong sense of ownership and responsibility. Collective insights were discussed, and from this, a new draft of ideal behaviors was developed. The draft set of ideal behaviors was shared with the entire indirect population during a week-long facilitated event. Each attendee was given an opportunity to flag anything on the shortlisted set of behaviors that they felt they could not live with. The objective was to reach a consensus. Feedback was gathered and the new set of behaviors and the "Essence of How to Live" these behaviors were shared.

The site's ideal behaviors were split into four distinct groups:

1. Not Allow Fear to Exist (this evolved in 2015 to Create an Environment to Thrive)
2. Understand My Impact on Others
3. Use Respectful Straight Talk
4. Enable Team

The journey started with each employee living ideal behaviors, driving a culture of empowerment and engagement. This allows the organization to constantly evolve and grow. The site's approach is "It Starts with Me." The ideal behavior's starting point is, "I will …" This demonstrates the personal commitment to live the ideal behaviors. This personal commitment is driving a positive inclusive culture within the organization (Figure 7.1).

After creating the ideal behaviors, a plan was developed with input from all of the line support team members to determine what work would be completed with the Product Builder population regarding ideal behaviors. An Ideal Behaviors Pyramid program was developed that consisted of behavior ambassadors from across the production area. These ambassadors instigated discussions where a pyramid structure was utilized. Each Product Builder gave input on how to live the Four Ideal Behaviors and

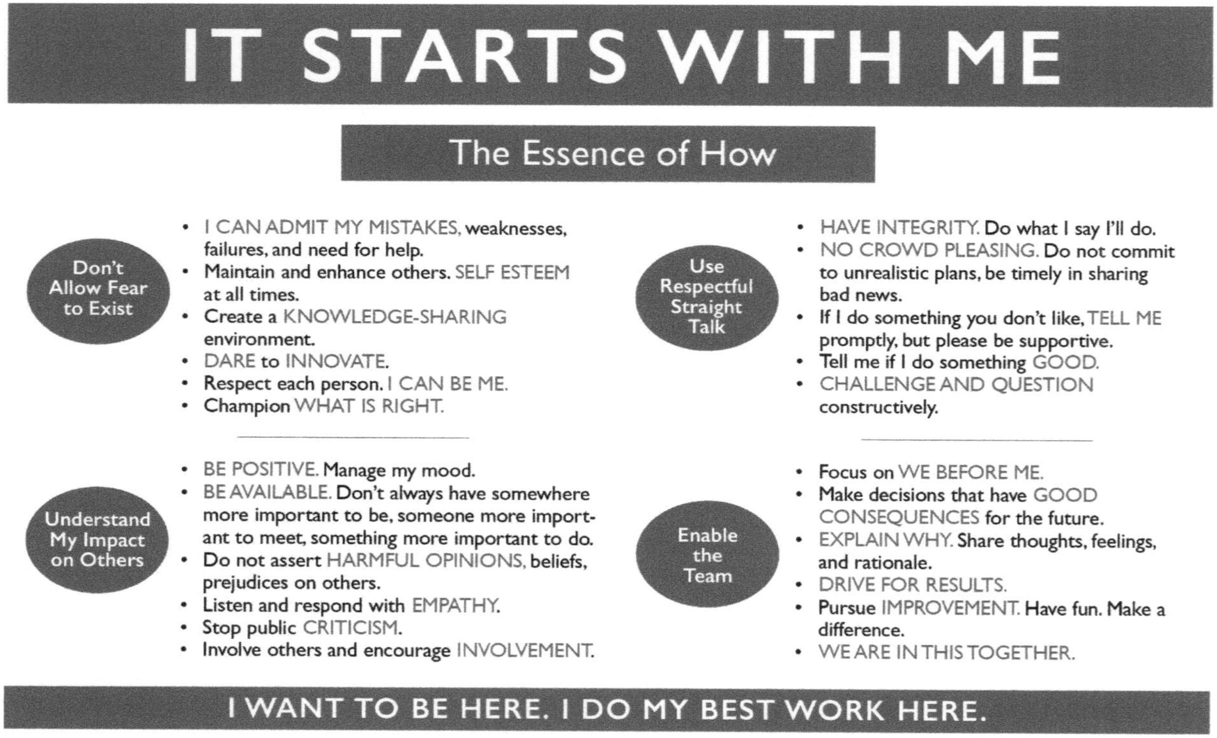

IT STARTS WITH ME

The Essence of How

Don't Allow Fear to Exist

- I CAN ADMIT MY MISTAKES, weaknesses, failures, and need for help.
- Maintain and enhance others. SELF ESTEEM at all times.
- Create a KNOWLEDGE-SHARING environment.
- DARE to INNOVATE.
- Respect each person. I CAN BE ME.
- Champion WHAT IS RIGHT.

Understand My Impact on Others

- BE POSITIVE. Manage my mood.
- BE AVAILABLE. Don't always have somewhere more important to be, someone more important to meet, something more important to do.
- Do not assert HARMFUL OPINIONS, beliefs, prejudices on others.
- Listen and respond with EMPATHY.
- Stop public CRITICISM.
- Involve others and encourage INVOLVEMENT.

Use Respectful Straight Talk

- HAVE INTEGRITY. Do what I say I'll do.
- NO CROWD PLEASING. Do not commit to unrealistic plans, be timely in sharing bad news.
- If I do something you don't like, TELL ME promptly, but please be supportive.
- Tell me if I do something GOOD.
- CHALLENGE AND QUESTION constructively.

Enable the Team

- Focus on WE BEFORE ME.
- Make decisions that have GOOD CONSEQUENCES for the future.
- EXPLAIN WHY. Share thoughts, feelings, and rationale.
- DRIVE FOR RESULTS.
- Pursue IMPROVEMENT. Have fun. Make a difference.
- WE ARE IN THIS TOGETHER.

I WANT TO BE HERE. I DO MY BEST WORK HERE.

FIGURE 7.1

Café Conversations at Boston Scientific are used to communicate current ideal behaviors, collaborate, and gain consensus on the right set of behaviors to live by.

a viewing event was scheduled, similar to the Café Conversation viewing event, where consensus was finalized. The "Essence of How to Live" was compiled and distributed to each Product Builder on site.

The ideal behaviors were guided by corporate values: Caring, high performance, meaningful innovation, global collaboration, diversity, and a winning spirit. The journey to create the ideal behaviors was driven by the people using the approach described above. In that respect, the inherent ownership sustained them into the future, demonstrating the principles of respect and humility in their creation, implementation, and daily adherence.

DEVELOPING AN EFFECTIVE PROCESS

After drafting and vetting the ideal behaviors you will focus on, it is important to create a process for assessment that not only provides you with an accurate and insightful view of the maturity of your culture, but also includes the presence of behaviors that align with respect and humility. The actual timing and logistics of the assessment vary from organization to organization and by the type of assessment you are conducting. You may only choose to assess specific areas or product lines rather than an entire site or division. Or, as with our discussion on using a survey, you may choose to focus on cultural enablers initially rather than tackle the entire *Shingo Model* right out of the gate. Regardless of the scope or timing of the assessment, the quality of the assessment and the robustness of the approach taken by the assessors is very important.

We have trained many examiners over the years. Each time, we spend time focusing on learning the *Shingo Model*, benchmarks, and behavioral best practices. However, the time we spend on the floor with each participant, reviewing the process of conducting an effective assessment, is just as important. When developing your own process, we suggest that you pay attention not only to the content of the assessment but also to the method of delivery and the proficiency of your assessors. To do this, here are some guidelines to keep in mind:

1. **Don't overcomplicate it.** The first thing to remember is not to overcomplicate the assessment itself. It is all too easy to throw in additional criteria or focus on more topics than the organization is

ready to understand and, more importantly, improve upon. Keep the process simple. This will not only help during implementation, but it will help your ability to develop your people into capable and confident future assessors.

2. **Use objective criteria.** It is important that clear ideal behaviors and objective criteria are used when assessing. Remember, you are already seeking to assess universal principles of respect and humility, each of which can have different definitions and behaviors associated with it. Spend the time to clearly articulate your ideal behaviors and the scoring system you utilize.

3. **Don't emphasize the score.** We have seen too many organizations over the years focus their energy on assigning a score or grade to each area rather than focusing on behaviors. If you emphasize the score, people will find ways to give you the score at the expense of actually developing the right behaviors. Remember, we strive to implement the principles of respect and humility because (1) is it the right thing to do, and (2) when we develop a culture of respect and humility, our business results follow.

4. **Recruit the right help.** It is critical that you recruit the right people with the right temperament. Just because someone is familiar with the principles of the *Shingo Model* does not mean he or she will be a good assessor. In fact, at the Shingo Institute, part of the process when evaluating a potential examiner for the prize is to first vet his or her experience in operational excellence and then to put the prospect on an actual site visit with an experienced team leader to evaluate how well he or she interacts with people, objectively assesses the organization, and interacts with the rest of the examination team.

5. **Tone is everything.** The tone used during an assessment is critical. The assessment is not an audit or an interrogation. It is a conversation where you actively encourage people to share the things they are proud of and those things with which they actively struggle. When conducting assessments, seek to model the principles of respect and humility. Not only will your people come to view assessments as a productive part of the improvement journey, but you will raise the level of trust in your organization while simultaneously raising the quality of discovery.

Example: University of Washington, Seattle, Washington

The University of Washington began its Lean journey in 2010 and built a culture based on engaging each one of their 1,400 employees in the F2 Division in the pursuit of daily kaizen. As with any transformation, understanding where they were on their journey and what gaps needed to be closed became paramount. A variety of assessments were used in different contexts and in different stages of maturity to help provide an accurate picture of the maturity of the organization, its teams, and its culture. Each assessment was built to leverage Shingo's best practices while also customized for the ideal behaviors created at the university and the expectations for system design.

When the organization began, the assessments were simple in nature (no more than eight questions) and focused on the fundamentals of system design and engagement. As the transformation continued and the organization matured, so did the assessment process. For more mature areas, the assessment grew to mirror a Shingo Prize challenge, albeit on a reduced scale. In the end, the process that worked for the university was to have a team of three people conduct an assessment over the course of two days, with ample time given to work around the schedules of the team members and to reflect as a group on the findings. The assessment itself was limited to 40 standard questions and the timing of the assessments ranged anywhere from 6 to 12 months.

The results of the assessment were put into a formal feedback report to the area. This feedback report was presented by the system and included focused recommendations for the next steps. There was never a score given to the area. The recommendations were then integrated into the strategy and incorporated as part of the tiered-huddle process. Implementation of the recommendations could vary from 6 to 12 months, and new assessments were not done until the area was ready for it. Finally, all improvements coming from the assessment were validated and, five years later, they continue to be in place.

UNDERSTANDING MATURITY

When assessing the maturity of your culture, we suggest using a similar approach to the *Shingo Model*. What is unique about the *Shingo Model* criteria is its emphasis on evaluating *observed* behaviors. Assessors observe and record actual organizational behaviors and then evaluate them relative to the behavioral benchmarks and a definition of ideal. This definition of an ideal is a level 5 on a 1–5 Likert scale. Level 1 means the behavior barely matches, level 2 means it lightly matches, level 3 means it somewhat matches, level 4 means it mostly matches, and level 5 means it matches exactly.

So how do Shingo examiners arrive at an objective score for a subjective principle like respect or humility? The answer lies in identifying ideal behaviors and the lenses through which examiners evaluate the behavior they are seeing. Again, the goal is not to make you Shingo examiners; however, in order to assess your current and future cultural maturity, it is important to understand the criteria the Shingo Institute uses to evaluate individual behaviors relative to the ideal. The criteria are represented in the acronym FISDR: frequency, intensity, scope, duration, and role.

- **Frequency:** How often does the behavior occur?
- **Intensity:** How passionately is the behavior exhibited?
- **Scope:** How much of the area/organization demonstrated the behavior?
- **Duration:** How long has the behavior been going on?
- **Role:** Who is demonstrating the behavior?

Armed with a set of questions aligned to the five key systems and your set of ideal behaviors, document the behaviors you see. Keep in mind that behavior is something that someone is doing. You will see more evidence of behavior that you will need to validate through questioning. Evaluate each of the critical behaviors relative to FISDR. This will enable you to draw conclusions on your current level of maturity. It will also help you see the gaps that need to be closed. Shingo provides a helpful matrix for this purpose (see the Behavior Assessment Scale in Figure 7.2). Remember that closing the gaps involves a review of the systems that are driving behavior and the tools that enable them.

Finally, it is worth noting that when evaluating the maturity of your culture, it is important to understand that while the Shingo assessment only scores the Cultural Enablers dimension slightly heavier than the Enterprise Alignment dimension, and less than the Continuous Improvement dimension, the engagement of your people is what enables

BEHAVIOR ASSESSMENT SCALE

This list of descriptors is the basis for assessing behaviors in an organization. Behaviors that match the descriptors would score at the top of the indicated range.

Lenses	Level 1: 0-20%	Level 2: 21-40%	Level 3: 41-60%	Level 4: 61-80%	Level 5: 81-100%
Role	**Executives** are mostly focused on fire-fighting and largely absent from improvement efforts.	**Executives** are aware of others' initiatives to improve but largely uninvolved.	**Executives** set direction for improvement and support efforts of others.	**Executives** are involved in improvement efforts and support the alignment of principles of operational excellence with systems.	**Executives** are focused on ensuring the principles of organizational excellence are driven deeply into the culture and regularly assessed for improvement.
	Managers are oriented toward getting results "at all costs."	**Managers** mostly look to specialists to create improvement through project orientation.	**Managers** are involved in developing systems and helping others use tools effectively.	**Managers** focus on driving behaviors through the design of systems.	**Managers** are primarily focused on continuously improving systems to drive behavior more closely aligned with principles of organizational excellence.
	Team members focus on doing their jobs and are largely treated like an expense.	**Team members** are occasionally asked to participate on an improvement team usually led by someone outside their natural work team.	**Team members** are trained and participate in improvement projects.	**Team members** are involved every day in using tools to drive continuous improvement in their own areas of responsibility.	**Team members** understand principles, "the why" behind the tools, and are leaders for improving not only their own work systems but also others within their value stream.
Frequency	Infrequent • Rare	Event-based • Irregular	Frequent • Common	Consistent • Predominant	Constant • Uniform
Duration	Initiated • Undeveloped	Experimental • Formative	Repeatable • Predictable	Established • Stable	Culturally Ingrained • Mature
Intensity	Apathetic • Indifferent	Apparent • Individual Commitment	Moderate • Local Commitment	Persistent • Wide Commitment	Tenacious • Full Commitment
Scope	Isolated • Point Solution	Silos • Internal Value Stream	Predominantly Operations • Functional Value Stream	Multiple Business Processes • Integrated Value Stream	Enterprise-wide • Extended Value Stream

FIGURE 7.2

The Shingo Institute Behavior Assessment Scale.

true alignment and continuous improvement to occur. Without engaged people, you cannot score well in either of the other two dimensions. Further, when looking at the relative influence of leaders, managers, and team members on achieving cultural maturity, the biggest and corresponding responsibilities are either directly or indirectly due to leaders and managers.

We only have to look back at our case study of TESSEI to see the importance of leadership in defining, modeling, and reinforcing a culture of respect and humility. It can be argued that although TESSEI's turnaround was due in large part to the continuous improvement activities of each of TESSEI's team members, without the vision established by Yabe and the expectations for a new philosophy of management based on respect and humility, the company would not have achieved the amazing results that it did.

ASSESSMENT: IT'S A CONVERSATION, NOT AN AUDIT

The most important part of an assessment is tone: The tone of the content, the tone of the assessor, and the tone of the assessment itself. It is critical that the process does not become an audit or an interrogation. To do this, think of the assessment as an opportunity for a conversation, and approach your time in the gemba from a position of humble inquiry. Edgar Shein says that humble inquiry is "the fine art of drawing someone out, of asking questions to which you do not know the answer, of building a relationship based on curiosity and interest in the other person."* When you do this, you learn more about your culture while at the same time building trust in yourself as a leader and trust in the assessment process itself.

---

* Edgar Shein, *Humble Inquiry: The Gentle Art of Asking Instead of Telling* (Oakland, CA: Berrett-Koehler, 2013).

8

The Impact of Enabling Your Culture

The only thing of real importance that leaders do is to create and manage culture. If you do not manage culture, it manages you, and you may not even be aware of the extent to which this is happening.[*]

—*Edgar Schein, Professor, MIT Sloan School of Management*

Throughout this book, we have taken the position that a world-class culture of organizational excellence is achieved through the careful design of systems aligned to ideal behaviors that are informed by the principles of Respect Every Individual and Lead with Humility. Make no mistake, every organization has a culture. The difference is whether that culture has developed by design or by default. In addition, when envisioning the culture you want, it is critical to understand the behavioral characteristics you expect to achieve and the results that should follow. Being in the business of building sustainable cultures of organizational excellence for more than 20 years now, we have learned that culture should not be built just for its own sake. A culture must be built to accomplish specific and measurable results—for the individuals in the organization, for those served by the organization, and for the organization itself.

To accomplish a cultural transformation and embed the principles of respect and humility in all you do, it is also critical that your vision for your culture plays a prominent role in your organizational strategy. You put yourself in a position to succeed by publicly declaring your intention to build a world-class culture and by relentlessly promoting the vision you have of what that culture will look like in the future. Culture must be a primary focus of leaders, and everyone in the organization should see and

* Edgar Shein, *Organizational Culture and Leadership* (Hoboken, NJ: Wiley, 1985), 20.

DOI: 10.4324/9781003425519-8

feel their commitment to achieving it and clearly understand their role in helping to build it.

That being said, this discussion regarding cultural enablers would not be complete without a review of the impact that comes from embedding the principles of respect and humility, balancing people and performance, and making cultural development foundational to all you do. As mentioned in the previous chapter on assessing cultural maturity, the impact must be measured both from the standpoint of cultural maturity and balanced business results. In the case of Gallup, the impact of raising the engagement of an organization's employees is clear. Better engagement equals better business outcomes. We have seen similar results with our clients over the years. For every improvement in the design and operation of key systems as well as the investment made in raising the skills and capabilities of leaders to model the principles of respect and humility, we have seen a rise in performance. The following case study illustrates how a public commitment to developing culture, combined with a focus on defining what respecting every individual and leading with humility and the design of systems, can yield tremendous results.*

TRANSFORMING CULTURE AT ABBOTT DIAGNOSTICS, LONGFORD, IRELAND

Abbott is a global, broad-based healthcare company devoted to discovering new medicines, technologies, and ways to manage health. As their mission states, Abbott is committed to helping people live their best lives through good health. Today, the company employs more than 113,000 people and does business in more than 160 countries. The company is composed of six divisions: Cardiovascular, diabetes, diagnostics, neuromodulation, nutrition, and pharmaceuticals and has been rated as the number one company for medical products for nine straight years (2014–2022) by

---

* For the purposes of this book, much of the story of transforming Abbott Diagnostics in Longford has been omitted. To understand more deeply how the organization integrated their focus on Cultural Enablers with the dimensions of Enterprise Alignment and Continuous Improvement, reference the complete case study: Sean Kelly, "Creating a Culture of Continuous Improvement and Sustainable Management Systems at Abbott Diagnostics Longford," *Global Business and Organizational Excellence* 36 (November 2016): 6–24.

Fortune magazine's Most Admired Companies list. Abbott has also been rated one of the Top 50 Companies for Diversity for 17 consecutive years.

The Abbott Diagnostics Division provides accurate, timely information to better manage health. Diagnostic testing provides information that helps in the prevention, diagnosis, and treatment of a range of health conditions. Abbott's life-changing tests and diagnostic tools put the power of health in the hands of healthcare professionals in all parts of the world. The Longford site is one of two Abbott Diagnostics manufacturing facilities in Ireland. It was established in 2004 on a 20-acre greenfield site on the outskirts of town.

Abbott Diagnostic Longford won the Abbott Global Environment Health and Safety and Energy Plant of the Year Award in 2009, 2011, 2013, and 2015 while finishing as runner-up in 2007, 2008, and 2010. It is a zero-landfill site certified in Environmental Management System ISO 14001 and Occupational Health and Safety Management System 18001 and Energy Award ISO 50001. In 2015, Abbott Longford was awarded IMDA Med Tech Company of the Year. In 2016, the site was awarded the prestigious Shingo Prize by the Shingo Institute.

Let's take a deeper look at both the Longford site's journey to adopt and mature the *Shingo Model* as well as examples of the systems they designed that help enable their culture and bring the principles of respect and humility to life.

THE JOURNEY TO EXCELLENCE

From the start, the Longford site adopted many of the systems and tools used throughout Abbott and its Diagnostics Division to ensure consistent compliance with global standards in quality and other areas.

Initially focused on the transfer of the manufacture of all key diagnostic reagent products from its sister site in Lake County, Illinois, Abbott Diagnostics Longford participated in the Abbott Diagnostics ATLAS Program from 2003 to 2007, which created capacity in Europe to better align reagent manufacturing capacity with sales.

To better utilize the increased manufacturing capacity of the Diagnostics business, Abbott's Blueprint Operations Program was initiated in 2008 and remained active until 2011. This program streamlined the manufacturing network configuration and significantly reduced complexity to best meet long-range plan and capacity requirements. These programs fostered a culture focused on delivering quality, compliance, operational excellence, and supply chain results, as well as project execution and the development of employees focused on continuous improvement.

The journey toward operational excellence started in 2009 when managers at Longford started participating in Abbott Ireland's annual multidivisional Leadership Excellence Program (LEP). The program challenged participants to choose projects that focus on culture and strategy rather than just cost improvement. The projects that were initiated through this program emphasized key elements of the Cultural Enablers dimension. Here are a few of the project examples:

1. The development of Longford site's vision of "world-class performance in everything we do."
2. The creation of site-specific behavioral standards that were developed by the employees and rest on the guiding principle of "treat others as you would like to be treated."
3. The establishment of an APPREC8 employee-centric reward and recognition scheme.
4. The development of the Longford site's strategy map and balanced scorecard, which includes stretch goals addressing finance, customer service, internal process, and people and learning efforts.

Given the site's stated vision of "world-class performance in everything we do," a new Business Excellence team was created and charged with establishing a roadmap to achieving world-class operational excellence. First, however, the team had to define operational excellence and decide what it meant by world class. After much research, the team decided that the *Shingo Model* addressed both concepts.

THE FIVE SYSTEMS AT ABBOTT LONGFORD

System #1: Environmental, Health, and Safety

As witnessed in their numerous awards for Environmental, Health, and Safety (EHS), the Longford site has developed a strong system with a commitment to all three elements. First, Longford's commitment to creating a safe environment for its employees is impressive. The primary goal for the site is to achieve zero incidents. To achieve this, they developed and implemented a plan called Moving to Zero. This program is heavily based on behavior safety practices as a means to be proactive in the approach to safety and eliminate the possibility of incidents, as opposed to just problem-solving once an incident has occurred. The Moving to Zero program looks at human behavior in relation to incidents and the behavioral adjustments that can be made to reduce them. The acronym CARE represents the four behavioral attributes that form the cornerstones of the program: concentration, attitude, recognition, and everyone. Moving to Zero training was given to all employees by their managers and relied heavily on interaction with participants through scenarios, role plays, and video analysis. Behavioral-based safety observations were also instituted in conjunction with the pre-existing safety audits.

In addition, the site committed time, resources, and organizational positions to reinforce its commitment to safety and achieve zero incidents. The site has a safety committee that is comprised of employees from across all of the site's functional areas. The committee meets on a monthly basis to discuss EHS issues and to review safety audit results and incidents/near misses. The site director and at least two other members of the senior management team also attend this meeting. In addition to the committee, there are two trained safety representatives onsite for the day and evening shifts.

In addition to its commitment to safety, the site has a strong focus on the physical, physiological, and emotional wellbeing of its employees. Longford has a site Occupational Health (OH) clinic that is administered by a staff nurse and supported by a contract doctor. The site also maintains an advanced Occupational Hygiene program that is directly linked to the Chemical Risk Assessment program. They offer heavily subsidized health insurance to all employees as a standard benefit and operate an Employee Assistance Program (EAP) in conjunction with their health insurance provider. The following initiatives further support employee health:

- **Active@Work:** The objectives of this initiative are to create awareness of the benefits of physical activity, to encourage all employees to become more active, and to provide a supportive workplace environment for employees to get and stay active. They established a Slí na Sláinte (Gaelic for "healthy way") walking route around the site perimeter and built a walking/running track called the Green Belt. They also organized onsite yoga courses, lunch-time walks, a 500K-in-a-day cycle relay, and participated in the Great Pink Run in support of breast cancer survivors.

- **Live Life Well:** The aim of this initiative is to improve employee health and harmonize health promotion across all of the Abbott sites in Ireland. A calendar of Live Life Well events is drawn up annually and health promotion initiatives are rolled out to all the sites at the same time.
- **Exercise Across Abbott:** Employees enroll on a team of 20 people and, over a four-week period, record their exercise hours. The objective of the program is to get employees to increase their exercise over that period of time. Teams that show an increase in exercise hours win a t-shirt.
- **Healthy Heart:** This site program raises heart health awareness in tandem with the ARCHITECT High Sensitive Troponin Assay. This included a patient story, an educational workshop on heart disease, children's coloring competition, and healthy food options and nutritious recipes in the staff restaurant, which received the Healthy Eating Award from the Irish Heart Foundation.
- **Sports and Social Club:** The site organizes sports and social events for employees and their families, such as Family Fun days, Christmas parties, football, golf events, Sports days, etc.

Finally, Abbot Longford continuously seeks out ways to reduce its effect on the environment. They have lowered the site's carbon footprint by reducing energy consumption and waste. Furthermore, they work to protect the local environment and natural habitat. Their work to protect the environment produced a 23-percent decrease in energy usage in four years while increasing production output by 68 percent. This was possible through the relentless focus on energy reduction projects, such as reducing air changes, resizing boilers, HVAC-free cooling, sensor lighting, blast cooler, and flue recovery.

The site has also taken steps to generate renewable energy by installing a combined wind and photovoltaic unit. This unit has a dual source (wind and photovoltaic) to generate electricity, which is stored in a battery unit incorporated into the unit. In 2014, the site extended its renewable energy generation further by introducing larger surface area photovoltaic units. These units connect directly to the site electrical distribution system and supply power in parallel with the incoming site electricity supply.

Up until 2008, the site sent an average of 45 tons of waste per year to the landfill. Since 2010, they send all waste, which previously went to landfill, for the manufacturing of solid recovered fuel. They have maintained a Zero Landfill Site status ever since. The site has also redeveloped its unused land into a biodiversity garden for the enjoyment of employees and visitors. This includes an orchard, two compost zones, a walking/running track, and employee allotments to grow vegetables. Furthermore, they have sown a wildflower meadow, which makes the site a more pleasant environment for all employees and visitors.

System #2: Training and Development

The real work to learn and understand the *Shingo Model* began in 2012 and all senior leaders at Abbott Diagnostics Longford attended off-site Shingo workshops. They were not only trained on the *Model* but also got to benchmark best practices in companies that had several years of experience in working toward operational excellence. In addition, the Business Excellence team organized an in-house Shingo workshop for Longford's middle managers.

This commitment to the training and development of its leaders proved to be a critical step in the journey. The workshop training was augmented with best practice visits to other world-class companies and Shingo Prize–recipient organizations in Ireland, Scotland, and the UK. These diverse opportunities to benchmark and learn from others clarified what "good looked like" in terms of a culture of continuous improvement that is built upon a foundation of respect and humility. They also formed the basis for future ideal behaviors and content for other training and development opportunities for leaders, managers, and team members.

To support employee empowerment and education throughout the facility, in 2012 Abbott Diagnostics Longford's Lean Six Sigma program was changed to focus on training as many employees as practical to a basic (Yellow Belt) or intermediate (Green Belt) level of Lean Six Sigma competency, rather than training only a few site experts (Black Belts) who would be primarily responsible for delivering improvements. This shift in emphasis helped create opportunities for all employees to develop their problem-solving skills. The site developed its own one-day Yellow Belt course to teach the fundamentals of Lean thinking and the Six Sigma DMAIC (define-measure-analyze-improve-control) problem-solving methodology.

Following their training, the students complete a project and make a presentation on the improvements and lessons learned during poster sessions that are open to all employees. A Lean Six Sigma awareness training program was also developed for all employees, and many managers have been formally trained in advanced coaching.

The focus on Lean Six Sigma training and awareness also extended to a program called Accelerate. With more than 100 active participants contributing from across all site functions, the Accelerate program further improved internal processes, developed workers' skills, and reduced costs. Through focused work stream Lean Six Sigma project activities, the program reduced manufacturing lead times by 40 percent, eliminated customer backorders, decreased inventory holdings by 10 percent, realized $2.4 million in annualized financial benefits, and increased transparency and flexibility.

System #3: Continuous Improvement

At Abbott Diagnostic Longford, respect for every individual in the organization is paramount, and efforts are made to harness the power of all employees by involving them in daily kaizen (continuous improvement) activities. The goal is a continuous cycle of generating, prioritizing, and implementing ideas that will yield improvement. To date, the ideas that employees have generated have enabled the company to make and sustain multimillion-dollar cost improvements and maintain an excellent compliance and safety record.

The company has also refined its employee suggestion schemes over the years. Established in 2011, an electronic Excel-based idea-generation system proved successful in capturing employee ideas, but it did not allow for interpretation, prioritization, and ownership for implementation. The transition to a daily kaizen card-based process addressed the disadvantages of the electronic system. Each team now has its own daily kaizen board where employees can post a card describing a concern (typically about one of their local processes) and a proposed countermeasure on the "Idea" section of the board. The teams review new ideas daily, and the proposed countermeasures are either accepted, refined through brainstorming, or rejected. If an idea is rejected, an explanation is included. Ideas selected for progression are moved to the "To Do" section of the daily kaizen board until the team can determine when the idea can be implemented and who will be responsible for doing so. Then the card describing the idea is moved to the "Doing" section of the board until the improvement has been implemented.

The visual and interactive nature of this process enables employees and managers to see all the ideas being generated and to track their status in terms of progress and barriers to implementation. It also enhances local engagement and ensures recognition for individuals and teams who have successfully implemented ideas. "Daily Kaizen Idea of the Month" lunch vouchers are awarded for the best ideas implemented locally and a gift voucher is presented to the employee with the best idea implemented at the site during the month.

The use of daily kaizen supports the development of Longford's continuous improvement culture by empowering employees to have complete autonomy over improvements and problem-solving related to their own work areas. Most identified concerns are readily resolved, and countermeasures are implemented by those working in the affected area. If the countermeasure is not obvious, then teams use weekly time slots dedicated to continuous improvement activity (CI huddles) to determine the root cause of a particular issue and to implement countermeasures.

The daily kaizen process is also used to drive full employee involvement in identifying and resolving issues hindering workflow and eliminating process waste. Daily kaizen promotes a culture in which improving the work *is* the work. This process may sometimes require the use of a 3C (concern, cause, countermeasure) problem-solving tool the site developed. When a particular concern is identified, its cause is determined through the use of such tools as cause-and-effect diagrams and 5 Whys analysis. Finally, countermeasures are determined and accountability for implementation is assigned. Knowledge sharing during management walks and value stream meetings ensures that lessons learned are effectively communicated throughout the organization.

System #4: Coaching

In addition to the formal Lean and problem-solving training available to all employees, the site also introduced a coaching program in which employees are assigned a coach to enable them to determine how to help themselves when they encounter problems.

Coaching has become embedded as a part of Leader Standard Work (LSW). LSW helps to ensure that all managers spend an appropriate amount of time during gemba walks to review and address area performance, coach employees, and encourage active participation in problem-solving. LSW not only details the task frequency and a timetable for action, it also outlines *how* the task should be completed and *why* it is required. This commitment to creating and reinforcing standard work for leaders with coaching at its core helps build trust, motivate employees, and drive cultural accountability within the organization. It also creates regular opportunities to teach and mentor.

System #5: Recognition

As mentioned previously, the Longford site developed the APPREC8 reward and recognition system as one of their projects aligned to cultural transformation. Under this program, any employee can write a thank-you note to acknowledge another employee whose behavior exemplifies the site's behavioral standards. The thank-you note is posted on an APPREC8 board outside the company cafeteria. Each quarter, the cards are removed and some of the commended employees are invited to an award event. Further, the site director chooses one of the nominees as the winner of the annual Site Director's Award. The recipient is recognized at an all-employee meeting and receives a trophy and gift vouchers. This scheme places a greater emphasis on recognition rather than reward and complements Abbott's other reward and recognition initiatives.

RESULTS

While the commitment to systems that enable culture is impressive, the results the site has experienced from transforming its culture are equally impressive. Here are some of the business benefits Abbott Longford has seen from their improvement efforts and commitment to their people and their vision for world-class performance in all they do:

- Nonconformance rate was reduced by 77 percent between 2007 and 2014.
- Lead times fell by 38 percent between 2011 and 2013.
- Inventory holding decreased by 27 percent between 2006 and 2014.
- Test volume output increased by 576 percent between 2006 and 2014.
- Cost per unit manufactured was reduced by 60 percent between 2006 and 2014.
- Test output per direct labor hours increased by 807 percent between 2006 and 2014.
- Energy usage fell by 23 percent between 2012 and 2015, while production output increased by 68 percent over the same period.
- The site has maintained zero-landfill status since 2010 when it began sending its general waste to be processed into solid recovered fuel (used as an energy source for cement kilns) rather than to landfills.
- High morale is reflected in the site's excellent employee attendance record of at least 98 percent, compared to a national average of 96.2 percent.
- Four hundred nineteen employees were promoted internally between 2007 and 2014, attesting to the success of career mentoring and coaching programs.
- Employees volunteer more than 2,000 hours each year to the site's corporate social responsibility initiatives.
- Winner of the Abbott Global Environment Health and Safety and Energy Plant of the Year Award in 2009, 2011, 2013, and 2015. Runner-up in 2007, 2008, and 2010.
- Awarded IMDA Med Tech Company of the Year in 2015.

The efforts of all employees to establish a culture of continuous improvement and sustainable management systems led the senior managers at Longford to apply for Shingo recognition. The assessment they had to conduct as part of the application process provided them with a world-class benchmark for gauging their facility's level of operational excellence. As a recognition of their journey and maturity in developing a world-class culture of continuous improvement, the site was awarded the Shingo Prize in 2016. They continue to use the valuable feedback they obtained from the Shingo assessors to ensure that all Shingo principles of operational excellence remain deeply embedded across the organization and continue to be reflected in the everyday behaviors of employees.

Since 2016, Abbott Diagnostics Longford has been awarded significant new business, which has substantially increased both the size of the facility and the number of its employees. Sustaining the site's well-established Lean management systems and culture of employee empowerment has become even more important to drive the ideal behavior and robust processes consistent with its vision of "world-class performance in everything we do."

BUSINESS CASE FOR BUILDING TRUST

Like many other recipients, BATO Shared Services Center in Costa Rica not only received a Shingo Silver Medallion in 2018, but it was also listed as a Great Place to Work in 2017. The Great Places to Work organization published a study* in 2016, making the business case for building trust in your organization. When analyzing the recipients of the Great Places to Work award, they found the following:

- The best companies to work for provide three times the stock price return (from 1998 to 2015).
- The best companies to work for have three to four times higher productivity.
- The best companies to work for have up to 25 times the rate of employee retention.
- The best companies to work for also have higher customer satisfaction.

---

* Jessica Rohman, "The Business Case for A High-Trust Culture." *Great Places to Work Report* (Great Places to Work, 2016).

Bibliography

Ahmed, Sami. "OC Tanner: Shingo Model of Continued Success." *Huntsman Teaching Case Series*. Logan, UT: Utah State University, September 2018.

Allen, Brent R. and April A. Bosworth, eds. *Systems Design: Building Systems that Drive Ideal Behavior*. New York: Routledge, 2021.

Bernstein, Ethan and Ryan W. Buell. "Trouble at TESSEI." *Harvard Business Review* (October 20, 2015): 99 (5), 1–16.

Blanchard, Kenneth. *The One Minute Manager*. New York: Berkley Publishing, 1981.

Blanchard, Kenneth, Cynthia Olmstwead, and Martha Lawrence. *Trust Works!: Four Keys to Building Lasting Relationships*. New York: William Morrow, 2013.

Cleaver, Eldridge. *Soul on Ice*. New York: Dell Publishing, 1968.

Clifton, Jim and Jim Harter. *It's the Manager: Moving from Boss to Coach*. New York: Gallup Press, 2019.

Collins, Jim. *Good to Great: Why Some Companies Make the Leap and Others Don't*. New York: Harper Business, 2001.

Collins, Jim. *How the Mighty Fall: And Why Some Companies Never Give In*. Boulder: Jim Collins, 2009.

Conant, Douglas R. "Secrets of Positive Feedback." *Harvard Business Review* (February 16, 2011).

Covey, Stephen M.R. *Speed of Trust: The One Thing That Changes Everything*. New York: Simon and Schuster, 2006.

Kelly, Sean. "Creating a Culture of Continuous Improvement and Sustainable Management Systems at Abbott Diagnostics Longford." *Global Business and Organizational Excellence* 36(1) (11/2016): 6–24.

Kelly, Sean and Peter Hines. "Discreetly Embedding the Shingo Principles of Enterprise Excellence at Abbott Diagnostics Manufacturing Facility in Longford Ireland." *Total Quality Management & Business Excellence* 30 (11–12) (2019): 1235–1256, DOI: 10.1080/14783363.2017.1363645

Kotter, John. *A Sense of Urgency*. Boston: Harvard Business Review Press, 2008.

Kotter, John. *Leading Change*. Boston: Harvard Business Review Press, 2012a.

Kotter, John. *Heart of Change: Real-Life Stories of How People Change Their Organizations*. Boston: Harvard Business Review Press, 2012b.

Marquardt, Michael J. *Leading with Questions: How Leaders Find the Right Solutions by Knowing What to Ask*. San Francisco: Jossey-Bass Publishers, 2014.

Martyn, Michael. *Management for Omotenashi: Learning to Lead for Passion, Purpose, and Performance*. Portland: SISU Press, 2022.

Martyn, Michael and Bryan Crowell. *Own the Gap: Building a Team-Based Daily Kaizen Culture*. Portland: SISU Press, 2012.

Martyn, Michael with Doug Merrill and Mark McKenzie. *Transforming Higher Ed: Implementing a Culture of Continuous Improvement at the University of Washington, 2010–2018*. Portland: SISU Consulting Group, 2019.

Meadows, Donella H. *Thinking in Systems: A Primer*. Vermont: Chelsea Green Publishing, 2008.

Monson, Thomas S. "With Hand and Heart." Speech presented at the Semiannual General Conference of The Church of Jesus Christ of Latter-day Saints, Salt Lake City, UT, October 3, 1971.

Nierenberg, Roger. *Maestro: A Surprising Story About Leading by Listening.* New York: Portfolio, 2009.

OC Tanner. "Appreciate Great in Culture Cloud." *New Hire PowerPoint presentation.* Salt Lake City: OC Tanner, n.d.

Papanick, Victor J. *Design for the Real World: Human Ecology and Social Change.* New York: Pantheon Books, 1972.

Plenert, Gerhard. *Discover Excellence: An Overview of the Shingo Model and Its Guiding Principles.* Boca Raton: CRC, 2018.

Prime, Jeanine and Elizabeth R. Salib. *Inclusive Leadership: The View from Six Countries.* Catalyst, 2014.

Rohman, Jessica. "The Business Case for a High-Trust Culture." *Great Places to Work Report.* Oakland, CA: Great Places to Work, 2016.

Shein, Edgar H. *Humble Inquiry: The Gentle Art of Asking Instead of Telling.* Oakland: Berrett-Koehler Publishers, 2013.

Shein, Edgar H. *Organizational Culture and Leadership.* Hoboken: Wiley, 2016.

Shingo Institute. "Cultural enablers workshop, version 5.0." *Powerpoint presentation.* Last modified November 14, 2019.

Shingo Institute. *The Shingo Model, Version 14.6.* Logan: Utah State University, 2021.

Shingo, Shigeo. *The Sayings of Shigeo Shingo: Key Strategies for Plant Improvement.* Translated by Andrew P. Dillon. New York: Productivity Press, 1987.

Sinek, Simon. *Start with Why: How Great Leaders Inspire Everyone to Take.* New York: Portfolio, 2009.

Sinek, Simon. *Leaders Eat Last: Why Some Teams Pull Together and Others Don't.* New York: Portfolio, 2014.

Torman, Matt. "Zoom Employees the Happiest in the U.S." *Zoom* (blog). October 2, 2019. https://blog.zoom.us/zoom-employees-happiest/.

Warrell, Margi. "Bill Marriott: Four Things Great Leaders Do Differently." June 25, 2016. linkedin.com/pulse/bill-marriott-four-things-great-leaders-do-margie-warrell/.

Womack, J.P. et al. *The Machine That Changed the World: The Story of Lean Production: Toyota's Secret Weapon in the Global Car Wars That Is Now Revolutionizing World Industry.* New York: Simon & Schuster, Inc., 1990.

Index

A

Abbott Family Science, 72
Abbott Fund program, 72
Active@Work, 101–102
APPREC8, 106
Appreciate results, 83
Assessment conversation, 96

B

Balancing people and process, 15
Behavioral benchmarks, 27, 41
    community, 28
    courage, 42
    empowerment, 42
    recognition, 28
    servant leadership, 41–42
    support, 27–28
Build excellence, 9–10
Business case for building trust, 108

C

Café Conversations, 89–90
Celebrate progress, 83
Changing perceptions, TESSEI, 57–59
Coaching, 79–80, 105–106
    US Synthetic, Orem, Utah, 80
Continuous improvement, 8–9, 77–78,
    104–105
    University of Washington, Seattle,
        Washington, 78–79
Continuous Professional Development
    (CPD) hours, 76–77
Cultural enablers, 8; see also individual
    entries
Cultural Enablers dimension, 85–87
    assure safe environment, 18–19
    balancing people and process, 15
    developing an effective process, 91
        don't emphasize the score, 92

        don't overcomplicate it, 91–92
        recruit the right help, 92
        tone is everything, 92
        use objective criteria, 92
    develop people, 19–20
    empower and involve everyone, 20–21
    examples, 100
    foundation of pyramid, 12
    ideal behaviors, 87
        Boston Scientific, Cork, Ireland,
            88–91
    importance of culture, 11–12
    lead with humility, 17–18
    learning organization, 21–22
    principles for, 15–16
    research on engagement, 12–15
    respect every individual, 16–17
    supporting concepts, 18
    understanding maturity, 93–96
    University of Washington, Seattle,
        Washington, 93
Cultural importance, 11–12
Culture cloud program, 83

D

Daily kaizen process, 104–105
Design for elegance and engagement,
    83–84
Developing effective process, 91
    objective criteria, 92
    overcomplicate, 91–92
    recruit help, 92
    score, 92
    tone, 92
Developing people, 19–20
Discover excellence, 7

E

Empower and involvement, 20–21
Engagement research, 12–15

Enterprise alignment, 9
Environmental, health, and safety (EHS),
    69, 100–101
    Abbott in Ireland and the Croí an Óir
        Program, 70–73
    Active@Work, 101–102
    Employee Assistance Program
        (EAP), 101
    Exercise Across Abbott, 102
    Forest Tosara Baldoyle, Ireland,
        69–70
    generate renewable energy, 102
    healthy heart, 102
    Hologic Costa Rica, 73–74
    landfill site status, 103
    live life well, 102
    moving to zero program, 101
    Occupational Health (OH), 101
    sports and social club, 102
"Essence of How to Live," 89, 91
Exercise Across Abbott, 102

F

Finding perspective, 39
Five key systems, 68–69
    coaching, 79–80
        US Synthetic, Orem, Utah, 80
    continuous improvement, 77–78
        University of Washington, Seattle,
            Washington, 78–79
    environmental, health, and safety, 69
        Abbott in Ireland and the Croí an
            Óir Program, 70–73
        Forest Tosara Baldoyle, Ireland,
            69–70
        Hologic Costa Rica, 73–74
    recognition, 81–82
        OC Tanner, Salt Lake City, Utah,
            82–83
    training and development, 74–75
        Viatris Damastown, Ireland,
            75–77
Foundation of pyramid, 12
Frequency, intensity, scope, duration and
    role (FISDR), 94
Frequent, 83

G

Gallup's research, 12–15
Give It Meaning, 83
Good safety system, 69
Great job, 14
"Grow Our Own" approach, 76

H

Healthy heart, 102
Humble leader, 38–41
Humility, 38–40, 44–45

I

I Am Accountable, 46
I Am a Leader, 46
Ideal behaviors, 87
    Boston Scientific, Cork, Ireland, 88–91
    examples of, 42–43
        adequate time, development
            activity, 43
        decision-making, 44
        feedback, 44
        share ideas, 43
        strategic goals, structured process
            and timely feedback, 43
    shaping the culture, 32
        agile and accountable, 33
        all for one AbbVie, 32
        clear and courageous, 33
        decide smart and sure, 32–33
        make possibilities real, 33
Ideal level, 1-5 scale, 94
I Drive Continuous Improvement, 46
I Make Timely, Fact-Based Decisions, 46
Impact of enabling your culture
    five systems, Abbott Longford
        system 1, environmental, health,
            and safety, 100–103
        system 2, training and
            development, 103–104
        system 3, continuous improvement,
            104–105
        system 4, coaching, 105–106
        system 5, recognition, 106
    journey to excellence, 99–100

overview, 97–98
results, 106–108
transforming culture at Abbott
    diagnostics, Longford, Ireland,
    98–99
Inclusive, 83

J

Journey to excellence, 99–100
Junior achievement, 72

L

Leadership Excellence Program (LEP), 100
Leader Standard Work (LSW), 106
Lead with humility, 17–18, 37
  behavioral benchmarks, 41
    courage, 42
    empowerment, 42
    servant leadership, 41–42
  examples of ideal behaviors, 42–43
    adequate time, development
      activity, 43
    decision-making, 44
    feedback, 44
    share ideas, 43
    strategic goals, structured process
      and timely feedback, 43
  importance of development, 48–49
  lean journey at Abbott One China,
    45–46
    our pledge behaviors, our
      foundation, 46–47
  principle action, Abbott Nutrition One
    China, 44–45
  results, 50–51
  shaping culture, 47–48
  through mindful leaders, 49–50
  understanding the principle, 37–39
    behavior characterization, 39
    common good, 40
    goals, 40–41
    growth and vulnerability, 38–39
    Shingo Institute definition, 37–38
    speech and behavior, 40
    vision of organization, 40

Lean, 3
Lean journey, Abbott One China, 45–47
Lean Six Sigma program, 103–104
Learning organization, 21–22
Listening is crucial for sound
    leadership, 51
Live Life Well, 102

M

Maturity, 85–87
Mindful Leader program, 49–50
My Work Matters, 46

O

One China Supply Chain Enterprise, 45
The One Minute Manager, 81
One-on-one coaching, 79–80
One Team, One Voice, One Goal, 46
Organizational excellence
  lean, 3–4
  Shigeo Shingo, 1–3
  the Shingo Institute, 4
  the *Shingo Model* and Shingo Prize,
    5–6
  the *Shingo Model* series books, 10
  Six Shingo workshops, 6
    build excellence, 9–10
    continuous improvement, 8–9
    cultural enablers, 8
    discover excellence, 7
    enterprise alignment, 9
    systems design, 7–8

P

Passion leads to performance, 22
Pay attention and celebrate
    accomplishments, 35
People's cultural preferences, 66
  connect to larger purpose, 66
  feel physically and psychologically
    safe, 67
  opportunity
    growth and development, 67–68
    make positive contributions, 68

part of community, 66–67
regular and honest feedback, 67
Performance, 83
Pride in one's work, 64
Principles for enabling your culture, 15–16
Problem-solving, 79, 103–105

R

Recognition, 81–82, 106
OC Tanner, Salt Lake City, Utah, 82–83
Reflections on respect and humility,
TESSEI, 63–64
Relating to others, 39
Renewable energy, 103
Respect every individual, 16–17
behavioral benchmarks, 27
community, 28
recognition, 28
support, 27–28
culture shaping, ideal behaviors, 32
agile and accountable, 33
all for one AbbVie, 32
clear and courageous, 33
decide smart and sure, 32–33
make possibilities real, 33
examples of, ideal behaviors
formal process recognition, 30
one-on-one coaching, 29
personal development, goals and
action plans, 29
safety, 30
suggestion system, 30
importance of safety, 33–34
lean journey at AbbVie, Ballytivnan,
31–32
overview, 23–24
owed and earned respect, 25–27
principles in action: respect at
AbbVie, 31
results, 34–35
understanding the principle, 24–25

S

Safe environment, 18–19
Safety Moment poster, 71

Shingo, Shigeo, 1–3
Shingo Guiding Principles, 6–7
Shingo Insight, 86
Shingo Institute, 4–7, 24–25, 37–38
Shingo Institute Behavior Assessment
Scale, 95
Shingo Model, 5–6, 10, 85–87
Shingo Prize, 5–6, 85–86
Six Shingo workshops, 6
build excellence, 9–10
continuous improvement, 8–9
cultural enablers, 8
discover excellence, 7
enterprise alignment, 9
systems design, 7–8
Sports and social club, 102
Support employee health, 101–102
Supporting concepts, 18
Support systems
best practices, culture cloud
program, 83
five systems, 68–69
overview, 65–66
people's cultural preferences, 66
connect to a larger purpose, 66
feel physically and psychologically
safe, 67
opportunities for growth and
development, 67–68
opportunities to make positive
contributions, 68
part of a community, 66–67
regular and honest feedback, 67
system 1, environmental, health, and
safety, 69
Abbott in Ireland and the Croí an
Óir Program, 70–73
Forest Tosara Baldoyle, Ireland,
69–70
Hologic Costa Rica, 73–74
system 2, training and development,
74–75
Viatris Damastown, Ireland, 75–77
system 3, continuous improvement,
77–78
University of Washington, Seattle,
Washington, 78–79

system 4, coaching, 79–80
    US Synthetic, Orem, Utah, 80
system 5, recognition, 81–82
    OC Tanner, Salt Lake City, Utah,
      82–83
Systems design, 7–8

T

Talent Management Review (TMR), 48
Target Zero program, 70
TESSEI, 96
    changing perceptions, 57–59
    getting results, 61–63
    overview, 53–55
    reflections on respect and humility,
      63–64
    transforming role of management,
      59–61
    Yabe, Teruo, 55–57
Timely, 83
Toyota Production System (TPS), 1–3
Training and development, 74–75,
    103–104

Viatris Damastown, Ireland, 75–77
Transforming management role, TESSEI,
    59–61

U

Understanding the principle, 37–39
    behavior characterization, 39
    common good, 40
    goals, 40–41
    growth and vulnerability, 38–39
    Shingo Institute definition, 37–38
    speech and behavior, 40
    vision of organization, 40
Understanding yourself, 39
Utah State University's (USU), 1–2

W

World-class performance, 106–108

Y

Yabe, Teruo, 55–57

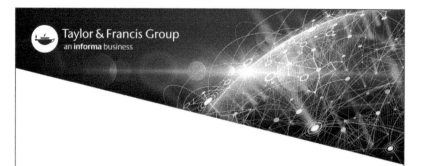

For Product Safety Concerns and Information please contact our EU
representative GPSR@taylorandfrancis.com
Taylor & Francis Verlag GmbH, Kaufingerstraße 24, 80331 München, Germany

www.ingramcontent.com/pod-product-compliance
Ingram Content Group UK Ltd.
Pitfield, Milton Keynes, MK11 3LW, UK
UKHW021820240425
457818UK00001B/2